INFINITE SELF

By Stuart Wilde

BOOKS:
The Taos Quintet:
Affirmations
The Force
Miracles
The Quickening
The Trick to Money Is Having Some

≈ ≈ ≈

Infinite Self: 33 Steps to Reclaiming Your Inner Power
The Little Money Bible
"Life Was Never Meant to Be a Struggle"
The Secrets of Life
Silent Power
Sixth Sense
Weight Loss for the Mind
Whispering Winds of Change

≈ ≈ ≈

AUDIOCASSETTES:
The Art of Meditation
The Force
Happiness Is Your Destiny
Intuition
The Little Money Bible (audio book)
Loving Relationships
Miracles

All of the above are available at your local
bookstore, or may be ordered by visiting:
Hay House USA: **www.hayhouse.com;**
Hay House Australia: **www.hayhouse.com.au;**
Hay House UK: **www.hayhouse.co.uk**
Hay House South Africa: **orders@psdprom.co.za**

INFINITE SELF

33 Steps to Reclaiming Your Inner Power

Stuart Wilde

HAY HOUSE, INC.

Carlsbad, California

London • Sydney • Johannesburg

Vancouver • Hong Kong

Published and distributed in the United States by: Hay House, Inc., P.O. Box 5100, Carlsbad, CA 92018-5100 • *Phone:* (760) 431-7695 or (800) 654-5126 • *Fax:* (760) 431-6948 or (800) 650-5115 • www.hayhouse.com • **Published and distributed in Australia by:** Hay House Australia Pty. Ltd., 18/36 Ralph St., Alexandria NSW 2015 • *Phone:* 612-9669-4299 • *Fax:* 612-9669-4144 • www.hayhouse.com.au • **Published and distributed in the United Kingdom by:** Hay House UK, Ltd. • Unit 62, Canalot Studios • 222 Kensal Rd., London W10 5BN • *Phone:* 44-20-8962-1230 • *Fax:* 44-20-8962-1239 • www.hayhouse.co.uk • **Published and distributed in the Republic of South Africa by:** Hay House SA (Pty), Ltd., P.O. Box 990, Witkoppen 2068 • *Phone/Fax:* 27-11-706-6612 • orders@psdprom.co.za • **Distributed in Canada by:** Raincoast • 9050 Shaughnessy St., Vancouver, B.C. V6P 6E5 • *Phone:* (604) 323-7100 • *Fax:* (604) 323-2600

Edited by: Anna Scott, Leigh Robshaw, and Jill Kramer
Designed by: Jenny Richards

Library of Congress Cataloging-in-Publication Data

Wilde, Stuart.
     Infinite self : 33 steps to reclaiming your inner power / Stuart Wilde.
        p.   cm.
     ISBN 1-56170-349-4 (pbk.)
     1. Spiritual life.   2. Peace of mind.   I. Title.
    BL624.W54   1996
    299' .93--dc20   96-32058
                                                CIP

ISBN 13: 978-1-56170-349-4
ISBN 10: 1-56170-349-4

08 07 06 05   19 18 17 16
1st printing, October 1996
16th printing, July 2005

Printed in the USA

Contents

≈ ≈ ≈

THE ANCIENT TEACHING
OF THE 33 STEPS

The *33 Energies of Man* was an ancient teaching. I believe it came originally from the Taoists in China. The 33 energies were said to flow from a higher plane into the earth dimension—a bit like a freeway built of light—to allow humans an exit out of the emotions and thought-forms of this evolution, into a higher consciousness. When I first heard of the concept from my old teacher, I found it hard to understand. The best way to explain it is that it is like a beam of light made of 33 strands, twisted around each other like a rope.

It is there, in effect, to give people inspiration and to help them on their sacred quest in life. It assists them in creating a consolidation of power, which in this teaching is called *Fusion*. Once the energy of *Quest* and *Fusion* have been established for a while, the 33rd energy comes out of that synapse. This is the energy of *The Initiate*.

I never liked the old definitions of the initiate; to me they always felt rather exclusive and elitist. I'm not up for the concept of "us and them"; I find it rather sinister and a bit egotistical. And I don't like initiates who allude to powers. They do so, I feel, more for status and cash flow than spirituality. If you are an initiate, I want to see what you can do and, if you can do what you say you can do, I want you to teach me how to do it as well.

In fact, through the teaching of the 33 energies, I discovered that the energy of the initiate is not necessarily one of a great wizard, or shaman—it's more one of transcendence. It comes upon you gradually once you have gone beyond the emotions and thought-forms common to this earth plane, and when you have let go of the ego somewhat and have embraced the Infinite Self within.

Yes, your perception grows, and often extraordinary things happen, but that is not the point of the exercise. The point of trying to attain a higher spiritual energy of this sort is so that it can set you free and liberate you from emotional disquiet—and so you can teach it to your brothers and sisters and set them free. That is the fairest way, in my view.

When I pondered on the ancient teaching, I wondered how one might translate 33 strands of light twisted around each other into something handy and useful that ordinary humans might use. I like energies that are "down here," that help you transcend ordinary things, such as your loopy mother-in-law who's driving you crackers. That's the kind of user-friendly mysticism I like.

Years ago, I decided to teach a weekend seminar on the 33 Energies of Man. I felt confident that I could translate the ephemeral nature of the ancient teaching into a practical method that might help people. So, I booked a fancy hotel in Washington, D.C., sent out brochures, and about 120 people showed up.

Thinking over the seminar I was about to present, I wrote the first ten steps out on little cards, but as I got to Step 11, my mind went completely blank. It was 7:30 A.M., I was in my room at the hotel, and the seminar was scheduled to start at nine. Panic!

As hard as I tried, I could not proceed from Step 10 through to the last three steps (31, 32, and 33), which I knew were *Quest, Fusion,* and *The Initiate.* I had a seminar that looked like a doughnut with a bloody great hole in it! I was about to get up on stage and admit that I was a complete twit, and that I'd invited a bunch of people to a weekend seminar that I couldn't figure out myself—a real bummer.

"Relax, dude," I told myself. I ordered breakfast: eggs, coffee, croissants, lovely stuff, all on a fancy silver tray. Now it's 20 minutes to nine, and I'm still none the wiser. I think to myself, If this energy is real, it will translate into human terms; if it is not real, there is no point in trying to teach it.

I picked up some of the hotel stationery and, silently to the great goodness out there that is helping us along, I said, "Great Goodness, dude, dudesse, whatever you are—custodian of the 33 energies—show me the rest of this teaching quick; otherwise, I am seriously stuffed."

A miraculous thing happened. I heard words go off in my head, and my hand began to write: Step 11, 12, 13...each flowed one after the other, all the way to Step 30. I jotted them down as fast as my stubby little fingers could manage. This is the book of the seminar that the Great Goodness kindly filled in for me after breakfast, at ten to nine, in D.C., 14 years ago.

Some of these concepts are those I have included in my other books, and if you have read all my stuff, then this will be a partial review of those ideas. But this is the only place in my writing where the whole concept is presented in one piece.

From time to time, I have found it very useful to go back over what I already know. Returning to simple things with a higher consciousness, you see that they are not as simple as you first thought. You remember bits that you forgot, and a new, deeper perception flows to enhance what you already know.

If you haven't read my books, the information will be new and fresh, and hopefully it will work for you. It has done well for a lot of people, and if you can get to the end of the 33 steps, and if you follow through with action, it will raise your energy, give you awareness, and set you free. Eventually you pass through a doorway to straddle two worlds: this one and another more spiritual, infinite world that is in an evolution alongside ours.

Of course, you have to have the desire to change and grow. That desire often starts out from a negative place—as dissatisfaction with your current circumstances or the people around you. You ache for an opportunity to slip away to something new.

Sometimes the great and wonderful goodness that is the invisible universe around us helps us by delivering a sudden change, one that marks a special turning point in our lives. In the film business they call it a plot point, when suddenly 20 minutes into the film something different happens that sends the story into another direction. When the current energy of your life gets stale and used up, the emotions, feelings, and discontent from deep within create for you a plot point. It often has spiritual or physical implications.

Maybe you get sick. For others, their plot point is whacking a tree—like at 70 miles an hour—that usually turns 'em around. Or there's a divorce, a death in the family, a bankruptcy, or something weird happens.

Generally speaking, when the ego is ticking along and it is pleased with itself, it won't consider spirituality or different belief patterns, ancient wisdoms, consolidation of power, personal discipline, or the kind of action that will turn a mundane life into a sacred quest. Usually you have to burn out all the ego's options first—and then whack a tree.

So when you read in the newspaper that four people whacked a tree last night, sad as it might be, know that what they were basically seeking was their Infinite Self. Of course, following these 33 steps is a lot safer. But some are in a hurry to discover themselves, so they whack trees instead. Sometimes we generate accidents in order to escape from an impossible situation, thereby generating the change we need; and sometimes we create accidents from a lack of balance when we are deep in the grip of the ego. So you shouldn't get emotionally upset. We are all infinite, and all events—positive or negative—are just part of our journey from ego to spirit. Some take a shortcut.

I did my arriving at God by the age of 28 because by then I was really bored, fed up, slightly psychotic, and totally dysfunctional. One day I did a very clever thing: I got rid of everything. I got rid of the stupid Rolls-Royce, my staff, all the hangers-on, and I gave what was left of my jeans business to my partner. I had an apartment in London, on the Chelsea Embankment, which is a pretty lah-dee-dah area. I remember thinking, I want to leave; I want to be free. No more *BS*—I want a life that is true and real and meaningful.

In the hallway of my apartment was an expensive set of mirrors. I called a friend and suggested that he send a guy with a van. "I'm going to give you some fancy mirrors," I said. He came along, unhooked the mirrors, and hauled them off, quite pleased with himself.

Then on the day I finally left the apartment—it was worth about $400,000 in today's market—I just closed the door and went. I didn't cut off the telephone or the electricity. Nor did I write to the bank and explain why they weren't getting their mortgage. I didn't owe them very much. I had loads of equity in the apartment, but I didn't care about the money—I knew the bank wasn't going to lose any cash; in fact, they'd make a bundle out of my departure, as they'd repossess the property.

I took nothing. I didn't even eat the food in the refrigerator. I left all my clothes and the furniture (except for the mirrors, of course), and I left the apartment as if I was going around the corner to the 7-Eleven. Walking down the street, I made a right turn off Chelsea Embankment, heading north toward Kings Road. As I stopped to cross the street, there was a storm drain at my feet. I unclipped the front-door key of my apartment and dropped it down the drain. That's how much I wanted to change. I was leaving. Walking out like that was the beginning of my spiritual quest. I had decided, "Hey, Stewie, it's time for something different."

Fortunately, I found a spiritual teacher who knew what he was talking about, and he started teaching me about Taoism. What's so beautiful about Taoism is that it teaches you to detach—not only from the world's emotions and the emotions of your family and the people around you, but it teaches you to observe and detach from your own emotions. It's almost like standing above yourself and watching what is going on rather than owning the whole opera. In learning to detach from your urges and disquietude, you become more clear, and less a victim of your own stuff.

The Tao is an interesting philosophy that comes from China, from about 500 B.C. It's written "Taoist" but pronounced "Dowist," which has always confused the hell out of me. The anomaly came about because the Western scholars who studied the Chinese language in the early days attempted to translate a Chinese sound into an English letter. They never really made up their minds whether it was "dow" or "tao." It's pronounced "dow" and written in English as "Tao."

So you've probably seen the Tao Te Ching or Dow De Ching in your local bookshop. It's a wonderful work—flowery and beautiful—but usually when you first read it you haven't a clue what it means. I must say I didn't either.

But the beauty of its philosophy is that, unlike a lot of religions, it doesn't have any rules. So Taoism was naturally attractive to me. Once you understand it, you find that its concepts are deceptively simple and inspiring. It takes you from the world of ego, glamour, and illusion, into the spirituality of nature and the Infinite Self. I was very influenced by Taoism.

The world of the ego is one of discomfort, even agony at times. You have to struggle to keep it happy. You can give it a new car to play with, a toy, some sexual experiences, you can get drunk and stuff yourself full of food, and still the ego wakes up the following morning to nail a list of things to your forehead, saying: "Hey, sucker, get me this, get me that. I feel insecure—I want more, a lot more stuff." The ego leans naturally toward dysfunction. It is tough to come to any kind of serenity in what the Eastern mystics call "maya"—the illusion of an ego-driven world.

Beyond the ups and downs of life, the physical plane is a glorious experience. From a spiritual perspective, there isn't any negative energy on this plane, only the illusion of negative energy. Let me explain. All negative energy comes from the perceptions and definitions of the ego. What we call misfortune, or a negative experience, is any contradiction of the ego's opinion. So if something happens to contradict you, you'll consider that you have suffered in some way.

You want to live a pain-free existence, and you fall off the sidewalk and break your ankle— there's a contradiction. You want to be cozy and warm, and it's pouring down rain. You want a simple lifestyle with plenty of money, but there are pressures at work, your spouse is giving you a hard time, the kids drive you crazy, the boss is harassing you, and now there are more contradictions to contend with. So what we call "negative experiences" are really only contradictions of the ego's opinions. Emotional pain is all self-inflicted. It doesn't make it pleasant, but once you can see that it comes from the ego's dogma, you can begin to heal it quite quickly.

I prefer a philosophy of life with no real absolutes. In other words, it's an illusion to say we have to be cozy, safe, rich, and healthy, or that we should live a long life—that's another part of the ego's legislations, isn't it? You may live a long time, and you may not. There's no point in living to a great age if you've lived all your life in a tick-tock prison that is a dysfunctional mess. (By "tick-tock," I mean the ordinary world of mechanical man.) It's better that you live a week or two as a realized, free, totally serene, loving human being than 90 years in the mayhem of the ego.

It's the quality of life while you're alive that matters. If today were your last day on earth, it would only be a tragedy if you hadn't experienced life properly—if you'd never allowed yourself to experience the sensuality of life, to really live it. What's the point, if life is just pain, anguish, dysfunction, and worry?

But if you've managed to reconcile yourself, spiritually and psychologically, if you have looked within and reclaimed the infinite power within you, then all of a sudden you can say, "Yeah, I've done it. I finally got there; I got the T-shirt, bro'. I'm happy to go on to another dimension."

Looking around at our Western nations, you can see that the quality of people's lives is going down the tubes. They are getting worse and worse, sicker and sicker. So you've only got two options. You can sit around and get physically and emotionally ill, or you can do something about it. The first step of this journey is desire. How strong is your desire? Will you consolidate and become free, and perceive the world in a different way? Can you let go of where you find yourself today? You don't have to go over the top the way I did and walk out of your house. But you do have to have desire, and you will have to act to change things.

You make the first move. Spirit never comes down to fetch you. It doesn't wander around saying, "Anybody here want to get realized? Anyone need to transcend?" It's not whistling in the marketplace trying to drum up business. It sits there, passively waiting for you to come and get it. So a part of your process is to reach up for it.

Put your arms up, reach out and say to that infinite God Force inside of you—in whatever way you want to describe it: Buddha, the Christ consciousness, Krishna, the Tao—reach up and say, "Hey, I want to change. I want to go beyond where I find myself now; because if I don't, I'll bore myself to death." You've got to want to change—that's the first move. I wanted to. I must say, I had a lot of desire and a lot of tenacity. A lot.

So if you're coming along on this journey, make the commitment. If you don't want to make the commitment, throw this book out the window. Once you make the commitment, it will gradually set you free, liberating you from much unnecessary weight. Some of these 33 concepts set you free immediately, and some of them set you free later on—three months from now, nine months from now, five years later—when you comprehend at an infinite level what they really mean, and you can see things in a deeper way.

It's like an onion. Peel off one skin, and there's another below it. You're always going deeper and deeper within, discovering new perceptions, and understanding life in a more meaningful way. So, desire to evolve, desire to become something different. Certainly, I had desire. Being brought up as a child in Africa and being forced to go through a rigid English boarding-school education and then on into a very uptight, rigid English society—that created the desire in me.

It didn't take me long to discover that I didn't fit in. In fact, I became a professional at being as eccentric as possible. It was my affirmation that one day I'd escape from the prison of tick-tock and the restrictive grip of a world that seeks to manipulate and control you. Of course, there are millions of people around the globe that don't fit. In my books, I call them "fringe-dwellers."

Fringe-dwellers are not necessarily hobos or hippie travelers, nor are they anarchists who are trying to blow up the joint. They are people who know there's something else to life other than ego, tick-tock, control, and the institutions. They're people who know and believe in a different reality—an alternative idea. Believing and acting differently, they extricate themselves from the common tribal emotions and make a dash for freedom. Right now they may still be driving a bus for the city bus company. But, in their hearts, they have moved to the outer edge of this human evolution, beyond what most consider normal reality.

I'm certainly a fringe-dweller, and you probably are as well, otherwise you wouldn't have been attracted to these teachings. If you don't know if you're a fringe-dweller, sit down and have a little "think" about it. I'm sure you are—like you're weird, man— totally weird. And I'm totally weird. And there are millions of us weirdos—all over the planet, making a difference to consciousness! Brilliant, really.

What happened to me is probably what happened to you. As I tried to fit, to mold myself into a three-piece suit and the English class system and the whole social structure, I'd trot off to the Royal Ascot races in a top hat and all of that; and there's the Queen moseying up the track in her little carriage, and everybody's so lah-dee-dah. I would laugh and think to myself, "What the heck am I doing here?" I realized it was hopeless; I couldn't do it. Fitting felt like failure—escape meant success.

The bottom line is, if you are a fringe-dweller and your mind-set doesn't fit, just agree to not fit. Why struggle? Sure, you've got to toe the line at work and show up at family reunions at Christmas and do all that "away in a manger" stuff. But in the end, in your heart of hearts, what you've really got to do is design a bridge that is going to take you from this side here, where it's all tick-tock and restriction, up Highway 33, that freeway of consciousness that leads to the domain of the Infinite Self. Once you see the world as energy and you see yourself as energy, once you have a desire to perceive, you automatically write a different evolution for yourself.

Think of it like this. Most people who are into consciousness raising and working on themselves accept the idea that life is created by them. If you're imbalanced, things go wrong. If you put out negative thoughts, you get negative results. These are not particularly awesome, earth-shattering concepts for people to comprehend. Most responsible people accept that they create their reality.

However, think of this. If you are inside the popular emotion, if you believe what everybody else believes, if you tick-tock along the way they tick-tock along, you are bound to wind up inside the group evolution of your people. Your destiny is their destiny. Because, if you're not thinking and acting differently, and you don't have an alternative perception of life, you've got to be mentally putting out what everybody else is putting out, so you'll wind up where everybody else is going.

I've asked people in my lectures, "How many of you are prepared to do nothing, just sit there and be dragged along in the collective common evolution?" Of all the places I've appeared, and I've played hundreds of cities, I think only one person ever put their hand up. He only wanted to know where the rest room was.

But almost everybody wants something different. If you think the way you've always thought, if you do the things others have always done, if you act in the same way, if you have the same emotions and beliefs, you're bound to wind up where everybody else is going. If you don't fancy that, you've got to change. You've got to select a whole different belief pattern, a different way of operating. Discipline. Silence. Respect for the spirituality within you. You can't have it both ways. You can't just sit and do "couch potato" and say, "Yes, that's a lovely idea, isn't it? Oh, yes, smashing, oh, yes! Very positive, lovely," and do nothing. You've got to be action-oriented, and you have to have desire. That is the key. Wishing to evolve, hoping to change, is not quite enough—action, dude! Take heart, and remember, you are not on your own.

I believe that the whole of the planet's evolution is wrapped into one consciousness; we are all microscopic bits inside that greater consciousness. Imagine the collective global mind as a huge hologram, each of us one dot in that hologram—you and me and all the others. If I change, it helps you. If you change, it helps me. Bit by bit, this conscious-awareness thing spreads all over the world, crossing religions and institutions, taking the heart of common people. It is the journey back to God. You can call it what you want because the God Force (he, she, or it) doesn't give a damn what you call it. Boogaloo.

As consciousness flows and spreads out, it changes people; we all wake up, and the evolution of this planet moves forward. So, if you incorporate two or three new concepts in your mind, and you raise your energy a little bit, you consolidate yourself, and then that helps other people—especially the people you come into contact with, who will feel your energy and see the difference.

We are all pushing energy in the same direction, trying to create a more loving, more conscious, better-put-together society for all our people. It may take a little while. It may take 500 years for everybody in the human race to go beyond being so assoholic. But hey, what difference does it make? If you're infinite, it can take as long as it likes. The fact is, it's cool to say to yourself, "At least we're moving forward, something's happening here, we're making an effort."

That's the whole point of these 33 steps—to generate energy for you. But you can't create a brand-new energy and still hold on to where you are now. If you want to flow down the eternal river of perception, toward your Infinite Self, you've got to let go of the branch you're hanging on to and let the river take you.

That means facing your insecurities and fears and really looking at yourself. Sometimes that can be a bit painful because what you see is piles and piles of *caca*—loads of it. And you say to yourself, "My God, I'm grim. I'm totally assoholic. I need to join Assoholics Anonymous. I am so assoholic it's painful." Then, once you can observe how assoholic you are, love yourself. Look in the mirror and say, "Man, this is one of the world's greatest idiots, but I love him, I love her, and I'm going to change them."

Think about this: if you were immaculate, a complete angel, totally over the top, perfect, you wouldn't be here. The whole point of our evolution on earth is to experience the crud and the muck and all the violence and dysfunction, and to accept it. Just getting into this physical body is a restricting experience. You wake up in the morning and there it is—180 pounds—much too fat! You've got to schlep it around all day—being in the physical, it's tough—hauling it, that is.

But you can't fight life. Accept the restriction and the negative vibes of the ego, and realize we are here to transcend them. If this place were perfect, we wouldn't show up. We wouldn't incarnate into a body. We'd look at it and we'd think, "Nah, it's too yawn-some—boring. I'm not going down into the physical; it's as boring as watching paint dry, there's nothing going on."

So, you are what you are. You have what you have, and everything is up for grabs. It can go either way. But first you've got to want to reclaim that Infinite Self within you, and so you start by calling it into your life.

THE CONCEPT OF
THE INFINITE SELF

Before we get into the actual *33 Steps to Reclaiming Your Inner Power*, let us discuss for a moment the overall concept.

As I said in the previous chapter, I was very influenced by the Tao Te Ching. What I like about the Tao is that it's not a religion—it's a spiritual and philosophical idea; it makes suggestions rather than offering dogma, regulations, and hierarchies.

The Tao Te Ching was written in about 500 B.C., in theory by a person called Lao-Tzu. Lao-Tzu means "old man," so nobody knows who the author of the Tao Te Ching was. It has been suggested that the Tao is a mixture of several different writers' work. Whoever compiled the work must have been a pretty cool editor, as he or she kept it very, very short.

I'd like to quote the first few lines of the Tao Te Ching and then discuss them with you. I'm going to use Arthur Wayle's[*] translation because, in my view, it is the definitive translation. The Tao Te Ching, Verse 1:

The way that can be told of is not an Unvarying Way;
The names that can be named are not unvarying names.
It was from the Nameless that Heaven and Earth sprang;
The named is but the mother that rears the ten thousand
  creatures, each after its kind...

---

[*]*The Way and Its Power*, by Arthur Waley. George Allen & Unwin Ltd., London, 1934.

When I first read that, my reaction was: What the hell's this guy talking about? I asked my venerated, spiritual teacher. One day I said to him, "Boogaloo, how'd ya get in touch with this Tao stuff?"

First, my teacher answered by saying, "Don't call me Boogaloo." Then he went on to explain that you can't really understand the Tao or the Infinite Self intellectually; it's beyond the mind. The only way to comprehend it is through heightened awareness and feeling.

He suggested that I rise at four o'clock—that's four in the morning—and walk in silence for an hour in the forest. So I began the discipline, walking in all types of weather. England has plenty of weather! I would walk silently through the forest in the dark, really not having a bloody clue what I was doing. But, strange as it may sound, having done that discipline daily for three years, I eventually got what the Tao was all about. It's true what it says in the first line of the Tao Te Ching: you cannot put a name to it. The Tao is timeless and immortal and has no definition. It is the essence of all things, it sustains all evolution (what the Tao calls the 10,000 creatures), and it's the underlying beauty that comes from the grace of God flowing through all things.

As I mentioned in one of my previous books, you can actually see the life force flowing through nature if your perception is clear and if you know what to look for. Wait till sunset, and get yourself into a relaxed state. Stare at the top of a big tree, and after a minute or so, move your gaze to the area of sky to the right of the tree. Stare approximately where the one o'clock position would be on a clock. Now, without moving your eyes from that point in the sky, move your attention back to the top of the tree. Don't move your eyes, just your attention. By doing so, you engage your peripheral vision. You'll see the enormous flamelike spirals of energy firing out from the tree in all directions.

As I said, this exercise is best performed at dusk, because bright sunlight and bright electrical lighting—especially neon lighting—swamps our visual perception of subtle energy. If you don't see the energy of the tree on the first attempt, leave it and try again later. It is probably because your peripheral vision is still underdeveloped; or perhaps you are not relaxed enough, so your brain cells at the time of viewing are oscillating too quickly. You have to be in a meditative state of consciousness to see the subtlety of life.

You might want to wait until you are on one of the fasts that I mention later in Step 26. Fasting also heightens subtle awareness. But once you see the life force energy that flows from a tree, it's easier to understand that the God Force runs through all things. It is the unifying power, the *raison d'être* for everything that exists. Gradually you'll understand what the Tao—the Infinite Self—can do for you. But to really comprehend it, as well as the angelic nature of your journey, you first have to release from the ego's somewhat tight, limited perception and accept your true spiritual power. When you are ready to release and detach and let go, you gain everything.

It took me a while to make the turn—to distance myself from the crazies that I used to hang out with and accept a more placid, yet powerful lifestyle. My quest was empowered by disciplines of every kind: I took on nutritional disciplines, fasting, the discipline of walking in the forest, I attended meetings with my teacher, and I read and studied and meditated daily.

Twenty-five thousand people were attracted to my spiritual teacher over the few years that he taught, and at each level of progress, the teachings and disciplines got harder and harder. After a period of about three years, almost everyone had dropped out; near the end, there were only 72 people left—one of which was yours truly. Eventually there were only three of us left. It was that tough.

The disciplines imposed by our teacher were difficult because they required you to be extremely spontaneous. So my teacher would phone and say, "There is a meeting next Wednesday evening in southern Spain at seven o'clock. Be there!" There was no question of: could you afford the travel expenses, get the time off work, were you happy with the idea, or was it convenient for you? It was a matter of "be there"! If you were even one minute late for a meeting, you got tossed out forever. There were no ifs, buts, or maybes; we were cut no slack.

I remember a session that was held in California, at Big Sur. The meeting was called for six in the morning. A number of us flew from London, including two South African friends of mine. We got to the hotel the day before and checked in. My pals were up early next morning and decided to go for a little walk before the meeting started. They arrived back at the meeting room at three minutes past six. They were not allowed to enter—in spite of the fact that they had flown all the way from London. That was the last I saw of them—on that particular path anyway.

What I learned from those experiences was that spiritual growth and the getting of a higher awareness is not necessarily convenient. That's why most never make it. They want to reach a higher plane from within the considerations of the ego and its limited consciousness—which often defines life into self-righteous, cozy little boxes, creating a self-indulgent energy that has the potential of a slug in a puddle.

The ego likes little boxes it is familiar with. But when considering an infinite consciousness, the first thing you have to do is burn the boxes. What Lao-Tzu was talking about in the first few lines of the Tao Te Ching—when talking about the Infinite Self, the Christ consciousness, the God Force, the Tao, the Buddhahood, whatever you care to call it—is that it runs through all things, it's everywhere, so it has no definitions.

Only the ego needs to define, discriminate, quantify, and measure things in order to create an edge or framework to life so it can feel secure and comfortable with what little it knows and comprehends. But the eternity of the grace of God flows through the life force of plants, trees, animals, humans, and all things. It doesn't have a boundary or definition.

You can define the position of a tree because there is a definite space around the tree where it is *not*. Here's the tree, and there's the space around it where it is not. But the God Force is omnipresent, meaning it's everywhere, it can't be defined. It is the "nameless" from which everything flows. If the God Force is omnipresent, it must also be God, because God is everywhere. The God Force and God must be one and the same.

You can work it out. There is a law in physics that states that no two particles can occupy the same space. So, if the God Force is everywhere, and God (He, She, or It) is everywhere, then God must be the God Force, and the God Force must be God—because you can't have a particle of God existing in the same place as a particle of God Force. Either you'd have to have a particle of God Force and a particle of God side-by-side, and then both of them are not omnipresent, or they would have to be superimposed upon each other, which is not possible. So the God Force and God are one and the same.

The act of defining life limits your perception of it. In the Tao, nothing is considered high or low, short or long. One could say, a journey is long because it takes you four hours to drive from A to B, but it's not long when compared to sending a satellite to Mars. And that isn't long compared to the distance from earth to the Andromeda galaxy.

Tossing out definitions of high, low, good, and bad is the first step toward grasping the indefinable nature of the Infinite Self. This can be a little unnerving for the ego because it likes the idea of my body, my people, my house, my car; I am here, and I'm not everywhere else. Of course, that is true in a strict physical sense, but in the realm of consciousness, your energy is bigger than mere concepts of my body, my life, my car.

As you expand your heart and go past your resistance to letting go, you comprehend yourself as an omnipresent, eternal being—one that dwells in a multidimensional state, timeless and immortal. Meaning, you existed before you came to the earth plane, you exist now in a physical form, and you will exist after you leave the earth plane—after your body quits in the earth plane.

The idea of the Infinite Self is beautiful, but it's hard for the ego and the personality to grasp. If I say to you, "Think about infinity," you can try to imagine something going on forever. But if I ask what does infinity *feel* like, you will probably not have a precise feeling you can identify with. You might say, "Oh, yes, Stu, I think I know what infinity is like." But thinking you know is only the first rung on the ladder.

First you sell the ego-personality the idea as an intellectual principle. Then through discipline, meditation, opening yourself up, moving beyond fear—through coming to a more compassionate understanding of this planet—you finally comprehend the Infinite Self as feeling. Then you'll be able to say, "Yep, I feel eternal, immortal, and infinite. I feel I am everywhere and nowhere. I dwell in the realm of spirit."

Next, it's important to grasp, early on, that spiritual growth is not necessarily convenient or comfortable. This is not only because you have to discard an awful lot of your beliefs and definitions—

things you hold sacrosanct—but also because you can't get to the Infinite Self without traveling back through the psychological and metaphysical reality of who you are and the memories of what you have done in this lifetime.

Looking at yourself can be uncomfortable. It's difficult to learn to control the ego and discipline the mind without it reacting. However, it's a vital part of the journey, and you have to raise your energy gradually, over a period of time. I don't buy the idea that something or someone is going to descend upon you one day and raise you up—a great guru, Jesus, or some angelic being—that they are going to touch you on the forehead, and suddenly you'll be elevated to a higher plane. I'm sorry if that contradicts your beliefs, but energy seeks its own level. Even though something or someone can inspire you or teach you, in the end the only way you will sustain a higher energy is to create it for yourself.

In the laws of physics, a subatomic particle can borrow energy for a millisecond, moving to a faster orbit around a nucleus. However, the particle can't keep that borrowed energy indefinitely. So whatever energy is borrowed in this second has to be paid back a split second later, and the particle returns (decays) to where it is comfortable, at the energy level it had before.

Spiritual growth follows the same rules. You can be inspired by a hymn, by a fantastic sermon, words out of a book; but you can only borrow that inspiration. In the end, raising your energy involves discipline, which means working upon yourself. There is no particular time when you can say, "I've done it, I've finished." Embracing the Infinite Self is a perpetual process, unfolding within you forever and ever. That is the only way you can sustain yourself indefinitely at a higher level.

≈ ≈ ≈ ≈ ≈

STEP 1

I AM GOD

The first of the 33 steps is called *I Am God*. You may wonder, "Who's this little twirp saying, 'I am God'?" What I mean by it is that you have to accept the idea of the God Force being within you.

Obviously, if the God Force is everywhere, it must be within you. But most people either have no concept of God at all, or they externalize God, creating a God *outside* themselves. Engaging the intellect to comprehend God, they are required to project the idea away from themselves. So they'll say, "This person is God, these ideas are God, money is God, glamour is God," whatever.

The God Force is within. Internalize that God Force and accept that it is flowing through you. When you perceive God as a force outside of you, you can't really use its energy properly. Once you internalize the force, and it is not just a vague intellectual concept of the God within, then you can move to actually *feeling* the God Force inside of you. At that point, a truly awesome power of perception and goodness enters your life.

There's a guided method to this journey of ours; it's not as haphazard as most think. I believe that the infinite you, that higher energy dwelling inside your being, had a vision of what it was going to be getting itself into in this lifetime. I don't believe that you came here by accident—that you suddenly plopped into a little diaper and thought, What the hell am I doing here? I believe that your evolution here on the earth plane is so powerful, so sacred, so spiritually dynamic and special, that the infinity within you had an overview. In the ancient teachings, it was said that the divinity, the Higher Self as some call it, could see the first 13 years of its upcoming earth life—not in every minor detail, but it could see the family you were going to be born into, your father's and mother's strengths and weaknesses. Perhaps it could see that you would be an orphan and be raised by your grandparents or live in an orphanage. That Infinite Self could see the genetic code and what physical disciplines or traits would influence your life. It could understand the mind-set and emotion of the tribal situation or culture you would find yourself in, so it knew approximately how your life would develop from the initial programming you would receive as a child.

This idea of the Infinite Self's overview of life prior to birth is quite radical compared to modern religious ideas, but it doesn't necessarily contradict them. It just says that the infinity inside you had a *perception* prior to your birth. It seems reasonable to me. As you develop awareness, you can see that people are not just a mind or a personality, full of tribal beliefs—or, of course, just a body. For the most part, they are, in fact, a *feeling*.

If you train yourself to see the subtle etheric life force from trees, sooner or later you begin to see it emanating from humans as well. Then you'll be able to watch their feelings oscillating back and forth. As you watch, you'll know a lot of things about them. If you were a person's higher Infinite Self, you would be able to tell, from even a limited human perception, "Hey, these tendencies are possible in the next three months, twelve months, ten years." But I imagine a human's perception is minuscule compared to the uncluttered infinite perception that resides inside you.

So if a human can perceive people's feelings and be aware of their probability patterns and destiny, how much greater would that infinite power within you be able to see what tendencies lie ahead—what difficulties, what strengths? Anyway, it doesn't matter if it had an overview or not. Here we are, and we'll make it into a fine and powerful journey, nonetheless.

Your first point of power is to embrace the concept of *I Am God*. At first glance, the idea seems egotistical. But you're not embracing the idea of *I Am God* to talk about it, or to show off and elicit the admiration of your Godlike qualities. Rather, you are silently internalizing the idea, accepting that the God Force is within you as a spiritual feeling.

Through this simple process, you connect yourself to the all-knowing, entering a mysterious and wonderful world that is usually beyond the ego's perception of life. This internalizing of the God Force can feel awkward, as we are brought up in what is either a Godless intellectual world, or we are taught to see God as a force outside ourselves. But it is your first discipline of power, so it is a necessary process.

If you currently have a concept of God *outside* of yourself, then mentally bring God home—allow its enormous power back into your heart. And even though you may not necessarily feel the infinity of the God Force within you as yet, at least you can imagine it there—visualize it there. This idea doesn't transcend any beliefs. You can still be a good Christian and believe in Jesus Christ, but believe in a Christ energy inside you rather than outside you. An intellectual concept of God outside you disempowers you, because what you're saying is, "I don't have a command of my destiny." This means that you don't believe you can create energy and make a difference. You can't get action oriented and change your destiny.

You can't believe in prosperity, act strongly and wisely, and get more money.

The second move in this process is to respect the evolution you find yourself in, which means accepting where you find yourself. Fighting against or bemoaning your circumstances, crying over the fact that you are not as privileged as others, crying because you are privileged and perhaps spoiled, being upset because you don't have all the physical strength or knowledge you think you need—all that is wasted energy, and disrespectful of the spiritual you. It's pointless, self-indulgent, and weak.

If you are to become a spiritual warrior and to honor the God Force within, you will agree to accept circumstances as you find them—remembering, of course, that almost everything can be improved and that things change. What you can't change, you probably don't need to change. You can just go beyond worrying about it instead.

Say to yourself, "The infinity inside me—that part of me that is God—loves and respects this human evolution of mine. It loves and respects where I find myself and my current circumstances, so I will do the same—even though the circumstances of my life right now may be less than best. All these things are a part of my evolution. I can transcend and go beyond them."

In pulling back from the ego's view of things and seeing life instead from an infinite view, you detach. You are not fighting yourself or life, creating unnecessary negative energy through your thoughts and feelings. In this simple and courageous act of acceptance, you begin an instantaneous healing process.

If you're surrounded by a bunch of incredibly negative, rather grim people—sometimes called relatives, or perhaps friends or co-workers, whatever—rather than fighting that ugliness around you and seeing it as a misfortune, love it. Look at the people, look at the job, your circumstances, the family, the tribe, your home, and say, "Thank you, God, thank you for sending me these teachers. They are driving me crackers, yet what they're teaching me is not to react. They strengthen me by teaching me to transmute negative energy into positive energy. Using these people, I will convert irritation, hatred, and reaction into at least a neutral energy of passivity or, if possible, love. These assholes are my venerated teachers. I am truly grateful to God for sending me so many assholes. Thank you for allowing me to be here on the earth plane. What an incredible experience. Isn't it fantastic that, almost free of charge, I'm surrounded by 55 assholes who are going to teach me a lot about myself?"

If you want to claim that infinite power, you will want to move away from the more rigid definitions of the ego. And, let's face it, the ego is rather self-indulgent, isn't it? It wants everything to be perfect, it wants you to be recognized, it wants life to be guaranteed, it wants things cozy, it wants to be paid more than it's actually worth. It wants a lot of stuff that isn't reasonable. To become free and activate the Infinite Self, you have to agree to ditch the dogma of the ego for a more fluid and open approach. Otherwise, you are perpetually stuck in the agony of the ego.

The first move is to at least embrace a neutral position, realizing that circumstances are neither good nor bad. The people who are driving you crazy are neither good nor bad. Your conditions may seem uncomfortable to the ego, but in effect they are neither good nor bad. They just are. Even if conditions are grim, from the definition of the Infinite Self, it's all a part of your learning experience—your challenge. It's a part of being here.

The concept of *I Am God* says, "I am eternal. I am beyond the definitions of the ego. I am beyond death. So, therefore, I will gradually go beyond fear. Fear is a disease of the ego. Negative energy and what we consider unpleasant experiences are just contradictions of the ego's opinion." (I talk a lot about that in my book, *Weight Loss for the Mind.* I'll deal with it here in the later steps as we talk about changing your view of the world.) Naturally, there is a great spiritual maturity in accepting where you are, who you are, and what you are.

Second, you have to accept that it is you who creates the major part of your reality and destiny. Okay, part of your destiny was prewritten when you got here—in your genetic coding and tribal heritage—then shaped by the things you were taught in your upbringing. But most of it can be changed, adapted, and modified for the better. So by internalizing the God Force, you begin to comprehend that the God Force within you can be expressed outwards—meaning that the force of spirit can be directed by you in any direction you wish, in order to change your life for the better.

You have been given the power. It isn't someplace else, up a mountain, in a building, or on a little cushion. It's right here in your heart. And you are not a little person lower down than it—one who has no power, no volition, and no ability. Once the God Force is inside you, and you can begin to accept the infinity within, your power grows. Otherwise, you have to rely only on the power of your intellect and perceptions of the ego's world, and you have to compete with other minds and egos in the marketplace of life. That's a sad way of going about things.

You are the God Force within. Affirm that several times a day. Say, "I am the God Force within. I can't necessarily feel it as yet, but I'm imagining it in the meantime." That's the first step in reclaiming your power.

Step 2

Expanding Your Awareness

For the second step on your journey, I want you to consider the importance of expanding your awareness. Most people, even though seemingly alive, exist in a surreal state somewhere between asleep and comatose.

Your initial awareness comes from the five senses, as well as from your reasoning, knowledge, and logic. Then there is the awareness you acquire from your experiences in this lifetime. But beyond your normal awareness is a more subtle awareness—an extrasensory perception.

It is vital that you rekindle, strengthen, and claim that extrasensory perception (ESP), because the language of the Infinite Self is very subtle; its promptings are not necessarily obvious to the conscious mind. It operates at a very fast, highly subliminal level of energy. Without a little ESP, you may miss a vital turning point in your life, or you may not see the answer to a problem that is holding up your evolution as a spiritual being.

Here's how the process works. Once you've internalized the God Force, and you accept that you are a part of an infinite energy that is all things—inside all—it follows that you are connected to all things. Think of it like this: external reality appears to be *outside* of you, but that is an illusion created by a finite point of view. A transdimensional being watching the earth plane—watching people's thought-forms and feelings—would see the earth as one molecule made up of various atoms, of matter, thought, and feeling. It would see all of our evolution *inside* the one molecule. From beyond the earth plane there would be no internal and external reality; there would be only the one reality, all of it internal. So you are inwardly connected to all things, seen and unseen, here and not here. Nothing is outside of you. Strange but true.

Over the years, I have experimented a great deal with entering the trance state. In that state, you eventually see the near-death tube. It's the tube that people describe as linking our physical world with the world of spirit. Having peered up the tube on many occasions, one of the things I learned is that the spirit worlds (those I have seen, anyway) are mirrored to the earth plane—meaning our left is their right, their right our left. But also I came to see that the spirit world exists in a rotation—that it is beyond our 3-D world in what might be a 4-D world or, more likely, a multidimensional world. I came to realize that our physical world, when compared relatively to the spirit worlds, is, in fact, outside in.

Now before you throw your hands in the air wondering what this Stuart dude is waffling on about, let me explain it to you as best I can. You have to remember that we only have words that describe a 3-D world, so once you get to rotations beyond 3-D, things get tough, language-wise.

Imagine a large beach ball that's pumped full of air. Take a few Lego bricks and figures from your kid's toy pile, and glue them on to the surface of the beach ball. Now, imagine that you could turn the ball inside out. The outside of the ball would be smooth, and all the Lego buildings and people would be stuck to the inside skin of the ball. A little Lego person living inside the beach ball would say,

"I am over here, and the red Lego building is over there, so the building is external to me." But in fact, everything is inside the ball—the building, the air, the Lego figures, with all their thoughts and feelings. The universe and our earth are outside in. We are all (from a spiritual, more distant perspective) inside the same beach ball, which describes our evolution/reality, and that physical beach ball is inside an even bigger ball, and so on.

Thus, we are connected to everything because we are inside the same molecule—and everything in that molecule expresses, to a lesser or greater extent, the God Force. The paper of this book has some part of the God Force in it because there is God Force in its atoms and molecules. That's not as much God Force as in something that's alive, such as a worm, and a worm has less God Force than a bird because a bird exists at a higher complexity of evolution. Humans possess more God Force than animals.

Once you understand that, and you understand that everything—even inanimate objects—emit a feeling, then you can understand that you are a feeling as well. A thumbprint of energy is the collective emotion you've developed in this lifetime, along with whatever amount of God Force you have mustered so far. You're not so much what you think, but what you feel. Those philosophies that say think and grow rich are not necessarily wrong, but they don't quite go all the way. You have to *feel* and grow rich.

Some humans have, over time, garnered a greater amount of God Force than you or I have. There are levels, but we are all connected. So you are this page, you are the worm, you are the bird, you are all things, and all of life exists inside you, even though they appear physically to be outside of you.

Realizing that everything is a feeling, you can begin to place your awareness into things to discover how they feel. How does a crow feel as it flies? How does this tree feel? How does the situation at work feel? How does the business proposal that the guy in the bar has just offered you feel? Is it crooked? Is it safe? Is it comfortable? So how do things feel? In looking at your reality in this way, you understand that you can push your consciousness into everything and figure out how it feels. These are the rudiments of an extrasensory perception. The system is not foolproof—sometimes your subtle perceptions get cluttered with your logic—but the more you use the muscle of your subtle perception, the more acute and sensitive it becomes.

From understanding that you're a feeling and that you're the God Force within, you have to grasp the idea that you can mentally *direct* that God Force. What that means is, you are a magnet for energy as well as a projector of energy. You live inside a personal thought-form that reflects your actions and words—but it also reflects your innermost hidden attitudes and feelings. Most don't consider their thinking or their inner dialogue to be of great consequence. To them it is silent and secret, and it does not seem to impact their experience of life particularly. That is not so. External reality instantly changes to reflect not only what you are saying and doing, but what you are thinking and feeling silently within. Everything you say, every thought, even a passing glance at people in the street, generates a minute subtle emotional response within you.

Do this: go to a busy street, and watch your reactions as people pass you by. You'll find that your mind comments and passes judgment on everything. You react to that judgment emotionally, experiencing desire, sorrow, or indifference. When someone repulses or scares you, you experience restriction. All these reactions come from just looking at people on the street.

Then consider the impact of your silent thoughts. What emotions do they create within you? When those thoughts are projected out into daily life, what effect are they having on what you see or on how life comes to you? Are those inner thoughts and feelings collapsing and destroying your life, or are they sustaining and building things up?

Next, be aware of your dialogue. It seems obvious, but most are not really aware how self-destructive their dialogue is. Negative people don't see themselves that way. They don't see how negativity is changing their external reality to fit their mind-set and thus destroying the quality of their life. Listen to your dialogue and watch your thoughts. See how much of it is bitching and moaning and expressing weakness, and how much of it has the God Force within it, expressing hope, gratitude, love, and well-being. Negativity kills you, never forget that. It's a weed that eventually chokes you to death.

If you believe in disease, you will imbalance the emotions affecting your overall feeling and hasten the disease within you. If you say, "This job is a pain in the ass," the infinite energy takes you literally and you get hemorrhoids. If you believe in lack, opportunities pass you by, money falls from your wallet, someone steals your car.

Ernest Holmes said, "Where your mind goes, energy flows." We know from our experience that Holmes is right. Whatever you concentrate on, you empower. So if you've been concentrating on negative or adverse things, if you feel overwhelmed by difficulties and dysfunction, you can be sure that they will all be in your "hall of fame," so to speak. Here's a statue to dysfunction. Here's another to frustration. And over there is one that honors struggle. Let's bow down to the god of struggle and give that 15 minutes of your reality.

The first point of awareness is to discipline your mind, police your dialogue, and cut out any deprecating statements—especially ones that destroy your energy and make you sick. If someone asks you how you feel, don't answer, "Horrible, grim, life's a nightmare." Instead, answer, "Fantastic!" It doesn't matter if your life isn't fantastic; that's only the ego's viewpoint. Spiritually, your life is fantastic, it's a great privilege to be here. I think it's important to remind yourself of that constantly.

At first your mind will be very strong. You'll say, "I believe...," and the mind responds, "No, I don't." You'll say, "I feel good," and the mind contradicts, "No, I don't." It's a tussle, but that is the challenge and beauty of this sacred journey. You are not necessarily perpetually victimized by your mind; you can push against it and change its programming. It's not a matter of wrestling with your mind, but more a process of quietly and consistently disempowering its negative influence. When the mind offers you a negative thought, say to yourself, "I don't accept that negative energy; I don't accept fear. I am love. I am positivity. Everything flows through me. Everything comes to me for my highest good." Thus, you start to replace the psychology that often creates so much destruction in your life.

As well as policing your thoughts and dialogue, you will want to keep an eye on the quality of your associations and actions. Stay away from people who discriminate and deprecate, or those who are involved in destructive or degrading actions. You don't need to judge them, but you don't have to be involved, either. Watch over your actions and make sure that you run your life in a positive and honorable way. Settle your debts, follow through on commitments, and treat people fairly. Don't allow your mind to suck you into actions that affirm weakness or that lower your energy and destroy your balance.

The other thing you should watch is the hidden nature of your motivation. When talking with others, notice and become aware of what it is that you are actually saying. What is your agenda? What subtle emotions are you experiencing as the conversation progresses? Underneath your words is the real you. Ask yourself, "Am I manipulating, cajoling, seeking praise or recognition? Am I trying to get my hands on this person's money? Do I pretend to like this individual when in fact I'm scared of them and I resent them?" And so forth. You'll be amazed what you discover.

Often, what you discover is that socially you play a *Mr. Nice Guy* routine, full of reasonableness, caring, and concern. Yet hidden behind this social-self is the real you, which may be vindictive, greedy, discriminatory, scared, self-obsessed, and possessing of a host of rather sneaky and ugly traits that make up the shadow side of you. When you uncover these things, you'll probably go through a dark night of the soul as you become aware that, deep within, you are not all sweetness and light. Once you get past the remorse of looking at your nastiness, you can, through awareness and compassion for yourself, heal that nastiness and transform the real inner you. Most of our jealousy and hatred and bitterness has its roots in childhood and our family of origin. Some of it comes from the competitive nature of our education system, which teaches children to contest against others—praising them for winning, and looking down on them when they lose. Nastiness and put-downs are a part of the system.

If you get in touch with your innermost being, you will usually be able to identify where certain derogatory impulses come from. If you can't figure it out yourself, go to a professional counselor and he or she will help you. Most of the satanic nature of our shadow stems from fear. As you embrace the Infinite Self, fear wanes, and your shadow side becomes lighter and more in control.

However, you do have to tackle the shadow. You can't come to the Infinite Self in the often phony cloak of just the social being. You come as you really are, and through awareness and the *yin* softness of spirituality, you see the reality of who you are. A lot of unanswered questions suddenly get resolved.

For example, holy-moly, whiter-than-white types are often racked with frustration. They are so good and generous to people, and yet they get very little in return. People are happy to take what they can get, but when the holy-moly gets too close, people flee. Opportunities appear and melt again, recognition is elusive, and life is always just out of reach. Why is that?

Deep within the socially acceptable holy-moly types lie what is often a sleazy agenda. It starts as self-hatred or a lack of self-worth, which they have to ameliorate and appease. A gracious demeanor plus good acts cover a poor self-image that seeks approval and recognition.

The savior archetype needs to have meaning in his life, and pretending to love and serve others is one way of achieving that meaning. Only a small percentage of that goodness is real and actually cares for others. More often than not, when viewing himself in the conscious state, this type sees himself as superior to others, distanced from the rabble by his holiness. Yet in the subconscious state, he sees himself as an outcast and inferior—hence, his need for approval. Feeling his hidden agenda, people stay just long enough for the handout, and then they flee. They lack trust, and quite rightly so; or they see the individual in a god-like way, which is how he or she wants to be seen. Ordinary people don't feel that there is anything they can do for a god, so they don't offer.

By discovering your inner nastiness and your hidden motivation, you see why your life is often laced with unnecessary contradictions and frustration, with the conscious part of you seemingly acting honorably, and the subconscious taking the very opposite tack. Notice and watch and remedy those negative impulses, and come gradually to a spiritually correct stance. This, for the most part, should be neutral toward others or, if possible, one of openness, support, and love.

One last point: when you die, you will see yourself in your total spiritual reality. It comes as one hell of a shock to some when they see that the spiritual reality of what they are is very different from what they think they are. Preferably, you don't want to wait until death and the next world to discover these things; you want to become aware of them now and fix them while you can. It is a terrible, sad moment if you die before you can make amends. You won't like what you see, or the consequence of that darkness.

Daily life is a symbol of the inner you. In using your ordinary five senses to their fullest, noticing and watching the signs, it assists you in the development of a sixth sense. So, as part of a heightened awareness, start demanding that your mind notice everything. Watch, look, count, and make a mental note of everything. If, for example, you enter a large hotel ballroom, within seconds you ought to know the answers to a dozen simple questions: how many chairs, lights, and waiters are there? What color is the carpet? Where are the tables, what's on them, and so on?

Constantly demand that your mind notice even the most irrelevant information. In this way, you heighten your awareness in the five senses; and in watching your surroundings carefully, you gradually strengthen your sixth sense, picking up more of what is going on. Heightening your powers of observation in the external world assists you in becoming more aware of your internal, visionary self. The universe is constantly talking to you and showing you things.

So, if you're walking down the street and something strange happens, stop, watch, and remember. If a black cat hops across your foot, does a somersault, and pees against the pub wall, ask yourself, "What does this mean?" The fact that you are coincidentally there at that precise moment in eternity to witness the cat's antics means that the symbol is yours. It's the external world talking to you. It is showing you things about yourself.

Thus, by internalizing the God Force—and by understanding that your Infinite Self and its inherent spirituality develops and grows only when you quiet the mind—you begin to see how the universal law of the God Force is trying to take you by the hand, show you things, and lead you on.

Life is a prayer; it's a dialogue. You are projecting energy and receiving energy; that is the interaction between you and the God Force. Watch that ebb and flow; watch your inner dialogue and the language of life's symbols, and offer up your simple human activities, your moments of silence, in a symbiotic exchange of energy and information, of asking and gratitude. The external/internal dialogue comes from silence, and it develops and strengthens through serenity.

In the ancient legend of Camelot, King Arthur took the sword, Excalibur, from the Lady of the Lake. That Excalibur is silent power; it's not the ego's power. It came from the placid lake, meaning it came from serenity. You don't have to be perfect to be serene. Tell yourself constantly, "I am serene and balanced, whether life is perfect or not."

Accept the gift of serenity, and bit by bit your emotions calm down. As that occurs, your spiritual power flows up from within, creating even more balance. It's a power that you will want to protect and hide away. You will use it to heal your body and to show you a transcendence that is not normally available to people. Now you must learn to guard the power—to protect your energy—and be vigilant so that you don't allow your ego to trash it.

It's a paradox of life that sees the ego, on the one hand, babbling away, trying to build itself up—hoping to generate gratifying experiences, exerting itself to get attention and to sustain its importance—and, on the other hand, generating negativity to trash itself and its dreams. Only the ego would believe that in moaning and groaning things might get better. Essentially, it's the small child calling for its mother to help it. I'll cry. I'll moan. I'll demonstrate the injustice of it all. Save me, help me. If I bitch a lot, will you give me something for nothing?

Expanding your awareness comes from understanding that everything is a feeling, and from asking yourself constantly how things feel. It's like a muscle that perhaps you haven't used for years; as you begin to ask, it will strengthen quite quickly.

Try this: ask the God Force to show you something in the next 24 hours, something you have never seen before—a perception, an intuition, a different way of looking at things that you've seen a hundred times before.

Then, watch carefully. Something unusual will pop up—and you'll see that the seeming external world is, in fact, internal—and it's talking to you. It loves you in its detached way.

Go on to the next section. If you have a minute, I'd like to talk about the courage and heroism of your life.

STEP 3

HAVING THE COURAGE TO GO BEYOND

S tep 3, *Having the Courage to Go Beyond*, is the act of letting go and allowing your life to enter into the spontaneous dynamic of free-flow. That means less structure, more trust, believing, and taking life as you find it, rather than trying to force it into a preconceived pattern and getting angry when it won't allow you to jam it into a corner in that way.

The ego is naturally resistant to letting go. It wants to hold on to its sense of power and to dominate your life and the lives of others. It needs to control because it feels insecure. So it may be frightening to let go, but in my view it is more frightening to stay where you are.

In the world of the ego and intellect, you don't have to develop blind trust. You can hope to rely on past experience and thinking things out and, hopefully, that works for you most of the time. But as a spiritual being, trust is vital. In the dynamic, exhilarating world of the Infinite Self, you're flying blind. It has no limits, so it's bound to carry you to unfamiliar ground—and that is what makes this whole process so fascinating.

The journey from ego to spirit entails resolving the paradoxes of this human existence. I can best explain it by quoting from a little book I wrote in 1994 called *Weight Loss for the Mind:*

> *We have to embrace infinity inside a mortal body.*
> *We have to believe in a God we can't see.*
> *We have to learn to love in a dimension where there is so much hatred.*
> *We have to see abundance when people constantly talk of shortages and lack.*
> *We have to discover freedom where control is the state religion.*
> *We have to develop self-worth while people criticize and belittle us.*
> *We have to see beauty where there is ugliness.*
> *We have to embrace kindness and positive attitudes when surrounded by uncertainty.*
> *We have to feel safe in spite of our concerns.*

The crux of the matter boils down to trust. You have to have the courage to embrace an idea, accept it, and believe it—*before* you have any real proof that the energy is there for you, or that the idea will work. You have to let go of that bad intellectual habit that says your ego-personality always knows best. By giving the infinity within you credence, you empower it to come into your life. It is almost as if you have to lose yourself a little in order to find yourself again at a higher level of energy. If you won't let go and trust a little, your ego-personality will constantly block off your inner power, and you miss the benefit of the subtle awareness and extrasensory perception that you're entitled to as a spiritual being.

We become used to overriding those inner messages, don't we? It's part of how the ego plays its games. The infinity within you is like a celestial wind; it will blow gently in your direction and assist you—but only when you quiet the mind and control the ego. People ask me, is it intuition? Yes and no. It's more than intuition. Spontaneous intuition is how it manifests in its early stages. Later, the dialogue from the Infinite Self comes through as all-knowing, instant information derived from heightened feelings. It grows as you focus and discipline yourself, and when you know and believe that you are infinite.

Once you can see the tick-tock world for what it is, the power of the Infinite Self joins you. It teaches you hour-by-hour, day-by-day, constantly showing you the subtle nature of things in a truly magnificent way. It brings you the people you need to be associated with. It shows you how to modify your belief patterns and which of those beliefs you need to sling off the cart forever. It assists your well-being and shows you ways of making a living that are less onerous and restrictive. The depth of its perception carries you from one stepping stone to the next.

It's a shame if you don't listen. While the ego dominates and holds on, the spirituality within you backs off and waits until you are done with the mundane logic of life. So, agreeing to listen is important; acting on what you hear is even more important.

It doesn't matter if, at first, you get things a bit mixed up if you're not sure what comes from the Infinite Self and what is from the mind. You have to start somewhere—that is the all-important first step.

If you don't listen and open up, the world you create via your personality and its preferences—and the perception you have of that world around you—starts to dwindle in energy. You use up the power available to you. The energy of the place where you live, your circumstances, your work, and the relationships you sustain, all begin to drop to a lower level because no new energy flows in to sustain them. Gradually you become less and less secure, entering into a stagnant dead-zone which is, in effect, the external manifestation of a tired and lifeless mind. Every day, there is less energy than before, less excitement, more boredom and irritation. Often this diminishing effect will be suffocating; you'll feel trapped. Life becomes a flat line.

In stagnation, danger increases; your safety and protection are weakened by the staleness that surrounds you. Imagine the dead-zone as a circular, flat piece of paper. Gradually, through negative emotion and the effect of restriction, the sides of the paper start to curve up; it begins to take the shape of an upside-down cone. The longer you allow the dead-zone around you to exist, the steeper the walls of the cone become, and the further you slip down the cone toward its inverted apex—the more you become trapped.

At the bottom of the cone, the intensity of your mind and the lack of energy and support in the circumstances that surround you are so great that you approach a situation of extreme restriction. Life closes in around you and, sadly, you may not have enough energy to climb out. The restriction of a lifeless situation such as this can cause disquiet and may result in dysfunctional or reckless behavior. It can lead eventually to hopelessness and an early death.

Agree with yourself, in a quiet moment of prayer or contemplation, that you *do* have the courage to be different. You will change, and you will fight the ego's lack of energy by embracing a few new ideas. You may get some flak from people around you because you want to change, but so what? In a stagnant situation, anything is better than staying where you are.

Next, have the courage to accept and weather the pain and aggravation that the ego will undoubtedly put you through as you try to disempower its government of your life. It isn't going to like what's going on. It will protest with logic and emotion and fine-sounding arguments, hoping to turn you around. When that happens, stiffen your resolve, and perform some discipline that the ego won't like. Throw yourself in the river at 4:00 A.M. every morning for a week. That should fix it, pronto!

In conclusion, to *The Courage to Go Beyond,* I'd add "the courage to be vulnerable." As you change and grow, the ego will feel assailed and threatened. If you have little or no resistance, you'll be fine; if you resist and fight, it will hurt a lot. So be courageous. Allow yourself to become vulnerable. Put aside the macho, dogmatic, insistent psychology that most people suffer from. Enter, instead, into the intense spiritual beauty of moving and flowing without necessarily knowing which way to go or how you'll get there.

Believe. Believe. Believe.

STEP 4

THE COURAGE TO ACCEPT SPIRIT AS YOUR INNER GUIDE

Step 4, *The Courage to Accept Spirit As Your Inner Guide,* is closely linked to Step 3, *The Courage to Go Beyond.* The first concept deals with releasing, entering free-flow, and becoming vulnerable; this one deals with moving effortlessly from intellect and logic to feelings and spiritual guidance from within.

The process is not so difficult. When you have to make a decision, rather than make it intellectually—Shall I? Shan't I? Will I? Won't I? mentally churning through your options—try to rely only on your subtle feelings. Open your heart to what spirit is telling you.

In any given situation, it doesn't matter so much what is logical; what matters most is asking what feels right. Once you have decided what feels right, move down that path gingerly; watch for any inconsistencies and problems, and adjust your actions accordingly.

If an idea is right, it will be empowered by your Infinite Self projecting energy outwards, and things will flow. If it isn't right, you may have to adapt a little or make a slight turn. But if that doesn't work and nothing flows, take it as a sign that the idea is wrong, that you do not have enough energy to pull it off, or that the time isn't right.

In passing, let me just talk to you about the difference between endurance and stupidity. When going for goals, you need strong intention and endurance. You have to take concerted action, concentrating upon your goal and putting enough effort in for a long enough time so that your goal is achieved. But when faced with a bloody big rock on the path, it should not be a part of high intention and good endurance to whack your head against it endlessly. Sometimes you'll find a way round the rock, and sometimes you can't. If that happens, retreat, come at it another way, or bag that particular route. Maybe even bag the stupid goal, if getting past the obstacle requires too much energy and struggle.

You have to think of yourself as a bank account of energy. How much are you paying out, and what is your return on effort? Sometimes you'll see that the potential upside in a particular situation is very limited, and the possible downside might include defeat, ruin, ill health, loss of a valued friendship, or suffering of some kind or another. So don't be obstinate. When faced with obstacles, work your way around them, or wait patiently; sometimes the obstacle disappears or melts away in time. Use your brain, not your skull. There is no heroism in whacking things with your head. That's dumb.

Trust your feelings, ask, and watch the signs all around you. You'll know how hard to try, when it's right to push a little harder, and when it's best to pull back. It's in the constant asking of questions that you logically don't know the answer to that you empower your inner guidance. If you follow along correctly, avoiding the ego's protests as much as possible, you soon find out that your inner guidance is always right. Gradually you develop enough confidence in the prompting of spirit to allow it to become your only guide in life.

Practice constantly. Let's say you want to phone a friend. Is she at home or not? Visualize your friend, and push your feelings out in her direction, searching for her. Can you *feel* her present at that location? Can you feel her soul, her character there? If your feelings say no, then don't call her. If your feelings say yes, then call. At the beginning, it doesn't matter if you're right or wrong. All that matters is that you get used to bypassing the intellect and the accepted view that says that you can't possibly find friends by just looking for them via an extrasensory perception. By going against the common logic, you are, in effect, asking permission to access a deeper, higher awareness. Your Infinite Self is linked to that of the friend you are trying to call; it knows if your friend is home or not. By asking it, and acting on its answers, you empower it. You become more courageous.

Lack of awareness has its roots in childhood. We require our children to endure the tick-tock influence of the education system—a system whose only reality is based in ego, personality, status, and logic. By the age of seven or eight, the inner knowing, which is gifted to you naturally when you are born, is usually squashed out of a child. We are trained to ignore the easy way of knowing things via our interconnection with all things, and replace it with a laborious method of learning by rote, intellect, and mind-numbing conformity and logic.

You need facts and figures as part of your education, but that should not become a high altar to the intellect upon which you sacrifice the subtle nature of your all-knowing. In order to win acceptance from others and from our schoolteachers, we tend to conform, and we become averse to risk. Gradually our metaphysical knowledge is lost, and in eating the apple of logic from the tree of tick-tock, we fall from heaven and lose our angelic nature. We're banished from the Garden of Eden to a much harder existence, with only the knowledge of the ego to guide us.

Eventually we learn to completely ignore what the spirit within is saying. The personality has made up its mind, and we follow along like good little drones.

Typically, your inner guidance says, "Turn left," and you ignore it. Suddenly there's a herd of buffaloes charging down the main street. After they've trampled on your foot and you're hobbling for months, the little voice goes, "Left, left, dodo!" And you'll go, "Yeah, maybe." And eventually you'll head off left. And there's this neat little garden and a bunch of nice people saying, "Where've you been? The coffee's cold. We've been waiting for you for ages. What's happened to your foot? What's that bandage for?"

We resist. I suppose it's partly fear and partly because the personality, and the ego therein, cannot bear to accept that there's a power within you that is more important and more knowledgeable than itself. However, when you think of it, all intellectual reasoning is mostly guesswork. Taking information from a past performance, one tries to extrapolate from that, guessing what course of action might be best for the future. It's a very hit-or-miss affair. The world is changing fast; what works today often fails tomorrow. Inner knowing is the best way of keeping one step ahead of a fast-developing world and changing circumstances.

As you begin to trust your inner guidance—call it the Infinite Self, a spirit guide, Christ, Swami Rami, whatever you fancy, it has no real name. As you start to trust, it leads you graciously, step-by-step. It will take you to the next person, the next place, the highest spot—it knows. How does it know? Because it is everywhere, and everything is a feeling, so it is all-knowing. As you concentrate and begin to rely upon it, it becomes stronger. A door opens inside of you. Click!

I've had people say to me, "Well, trusting is frightening."

"Yes," I reply. "It's supposed to be. That's the nature of this sacred quest."

In fact, it is only your personality that's frightened. The *real* you is eternal and immortal. It can't be frightened or sick or confused. It lives in a perfect dimension of exquisite beauty. So, if you have a fear of letting go, start getting a grip on your personality by talking to it and helping it through the experience. Talk to it like you would a child, saying, "Hello, little ego, I know you're scared of letting go. I know you worry about me quitting this dumb job in case there isn't another one. But I'm eternal. I'm abundant. I'm infinite. I know there's something better up ahead because my Infinite Self can feel it. So don't worry, little guy. We'll be just fine."

This sacred and holy journey—the journey away from ego toward the Infinite Self—is a journey through a fog. You're only going to be able to see a few steps in front of you. If you can see down the path six months, a year, five years, twenty years, here's my pension, here's my retirement, here's my destiny—*yawn, yawn,* you are deeply in the clutch of the demons of tick-tock, a prisoner in the world of the ego that sets up safe, boring rhythms to keep itself comfortable. So it leans toward the mind-numbing— Monday's wash day, Tuesday's meat loaf, Wednesday's ten-pin bowling, and we'll drone on from there.

You'll know if you are growing and moving toward the Infinite Self by the fact that you have more choices. Things will be less definite. You won't see so far into the future. Your time horizon shortens, and life becomes more immediate. All you'll ever know is: "Hey, I feel fine right now." So trust is important.

Here's an exercise you can do, and I'm sure you can invent half-a-dozen others. Next time you have a free evening, try blindfolding yourself. I'm presuming here that you aren't blind—if you are, you don't need this exercise as you'll know it through and through.

Okay, the rest of you do this: spend the evening blindfolded. You may want to walk around the house first and secure any areas that might be unsafe. You don't want to chuck yourself down the cellar steps just to discover your Infinite Self!

Plan for the exercise to last about three hours. It's important that it lasts long enough for your ego to give up control. The object of the exercise is to disempower the ego's dominance and for you to operate just through feelings. So, fix your dinner, then blindfold yourself and wander around the house as you normally would.

As you contend with the temporary loss of sight, you might get frustrated or scared or bored; your ego may react to its loss of control. Be determined, push against its resistance, and follow through to the end. You are trying to develop confidence in allowing your feelings to guide you.

There is a process we do in a seminar called *Wildefire,* which I give once a year for men, whereby we take the lads blindfolded up a thickly forested hill. They have to carry two eggs, which symbolize the weight of responsibilities a man takes on in life. The men follow the sound of a drum for about a hour while making sure they don't break the eggs.

At first, they experience serious amounts of whacking their heads on tree limbs and falling over things. Some become incapacitated by the loss of sight, and gradually they become more and more distanced from the drum. It's symbolic of their losing touch with their Infinite Self. As soon as they resolve their incapacity— and stop trying to be clever dicks and thinking the process out— they discover that they can feel where the trees are, and they begin to move through the undergrowth with more assurance and less pain! By the end, they are walking at almost a normal pace.

Sometimes, if the drummer daydreams a little, the blindfolded men catch up with him before the exercise has run its full course. It never ceases to amaze me how people can develop an extrasensory perception at incredible speed once they agree to its existence, and once they begin to call upon that part of their perception.

So the courage of accepting spirit as your guide does not require great fortitude. It's just being courageous enough to step away from the handrail of life, which delineates the mind-set of tick-tock, and walk a little way into the unknown. Personally, I find the unknown interesting. You meet people and travel to different places; deals and opportunities pop up. You come to expect the unexpected.

Here are a couple of other things to remember to get your inner guidance working a bit better for you:

First: to get the ego to back off, you have to shove against its comfort zones. So, pick stuff it doesn't like. If, say, public speaking terrifies you, agree to give a speech. If heights bother you, go parachuting. If the dark bothers you, walk in the forest at night like I did. Each week, devise one thing that you will use to challenge yourself—to push the envelope of your resistance, make that your greater strengthening.

Second: discipline yourself to remain mentally in the now. Don't allow the mind to daydream, and don't worry about the future. Sure, you can make plans for future things that need to be organized today, but don't future-think too much. Stay centered in the eternal present. Working on trusting and exercising the muscle of your perception, it grows quickly.

STEP 5

ACCEPTING NEGATIVITY AS A LEARNING EXPERIENCE

S tep 5 embraces changing one's attitude to what seems like misfortune or negativity. *Negativity* is a term that has cropped up in recent years and describes the unpleasant experiences of life. Most people react to misfortune in a predictable way.

The ego has rules and regulations. From these come its desires, needs, opinions, beliefs, and fears. Any time the ego perceives negativity, it will react. It will react from arrogance or righteousness, or it will react from its sense of insecurity or from a sense of injustice because its status quo is being assailed; or perhaps its power is being diminished in some way.

Take poverty—poverty is a good example of what the ego usually thinks of as a negative energy. Poverty in the Western world, more often that not, comes from a lack of concerted energy. Given our welfare system and social security apparatus and the fact that there are hundreds, if not thousands, of "help wanted" ads in the paper every day, anybody who desperately needed a job today could get one, even if it's serving hamburgers. The idea that people have to beg in the street, starving as a result of some fault of our society, is not necessary in our Western world.

When you look at people begging and you react to their lack by expressing emotion, you're expressing the indignation of the ego. The ego's view is self-centered and laced with its own fears. It says, "Look at all these poor people. They should have abundance and cars, VCRs, importance, and homes. They should be provided for so that their life is cozy and effortless; they should have all the things my ego feels are vital for my well-being and security."

Here on the planet, you have to create energy if you want things—concerted energy that makes you more valuable to the other citizens on the planet, who are going to pay you for your contribution to their well-being.

Looking at the world in the finite, emotional ego sense, we judge it, making it wrong. It's only the ego's opinion that life should be cozy and effortless, and everybody should have plenty of money. That isn't necessarily the case. When you look at the world from the ego's view, a lot of things seem preposterous. But the beggar on the street is not just ego, personality, and body. He or she is infinite, and inside that body is an eternal evolution. You don't know that poverty isn't something the beggar needs to experience to understand himself, to grow. Perhaps he needs to fall to his lowest ebb to come to the conclusion, "Hey, if I sit in the dirt here, I don't get very far. What I really need to do is stand up, brush myself off, and put out some energy."

Of course, you must have compassion for the weaker members of society, and you should do what you can to assist. But there is a difference between, say, just giving a person money and actually motivating him, thereby teaching him a skill so he can earn a living and enhance his well-being for the rest of his life.

Our society is organized in such a way politically that we underwrite weakness. That's why we have a whole media system designed for cranking people's indignation. It's a political expedient that forces us to invest in enormously complex and expensive systems to make sure that every citizen will be provided for even if they put out no effort. It appeals to the ego, wins votes, and bankrupts the country.

I have been criticized in the past for my attitude, but I prefer the long-term spiritual view, not the short-term emotional expedient. Rather than being sucked into the common emotion of misfortune, you can detach and see things as they are. You can ponder the long-term consequence of our political judgments; you'll soon see that the indulgence of handouts destroys a nation financially and spiritually.

Just to give you a quick example of this alternative perspective, let's look at the situation in Great Britain. The government receives 74 billion pounds annually in income tax deducted from the workers of the nation, and it pays out 76 billion pounds in social security handouts. That sum does not include the cost of the national health system. Providing free health care and medicine to 58 million people is enormously expensive.

As a result of these handouts, Great Britain doesn't really have any extremes of poverty, and all the non-tiers are well coddled and looked after to at least a minimum standard. In theory, that should work well. In practice, it creates an enormous underclass of people who are indolent and self-righteous, and who are often dishonestly milking the system, expecting life on a platter.

This crazy system leads to more and more national debt, less and less energy; more drugs, violence and crime, and all the common diseases of a rampant ego. It also creates resentment and hatred on the part of the workers who don't enjoy being milked to sustain the able-bodied who are paid for doing nothing. Worst of all, the overspending and indulgence affects prices and interest rates. Everything is more expensive for everyone, and it gradually bankrupts the country.

As the government becomes more and more impoverished, it soon turns on the citizens. It begins to feed off its people for its own political survival. The government becomes a predator, not a protector, of the people.

America is a good example of this. As the country has gone more and more into debt, the government has turned on its people and is doing its best to repossess as much of their wealth by terror or force or whatever means it can. In less than a generation, what was seen as a benign, friendly institution that had the best interests of its citizens at heart, has changed to an autocratic, authoritarian, neo-Fascist police state.

The oppression by the American government of its people is a terrible thing because it crushes the very reason for America's success—its inventiveness and its positive sense of "can do" and hope.

For people to experience their spirituality and to grow and learn from their time on earth, they need the level playing field of a fair and stable democracy. Under the current policies, our Western nations are heading for eventual collapse and financial ruin. With that comes anarchy, fascism, fear, and lots of ugly manifestations of a national ego out of control, which inevitably comes about when the self-indulgent, cushy ride is eventually over. So my view is one of trying to help people grow stronger, but not to underwrite their disease. We need to keep our countries afloat. If we give in to the political ego, it will eventually sink the playing field of our spiritual evolution. It will crush our hope, and we'll experience a terrible hardship because of that. So you can coddle society and give millions a free ride—and have the nation, as we know it now, last 25 more years. Or, you can teach people to control the ego, to put out energy, and become self-sufficient—and the democracy can last forever. The long-term view is my choice.

It's important not to get sucked into the short-term emotion. You should remember that when you look at negative energy, you're only looking at events or circumstances that contradict the ego. So the ego says, "I want to live forever," and the body dies. We consider that a negative event, and we say, "Harry died." And we all take a moment to remember Harry. But Harry isn't dead; he's infinite. You'll never be more alive than the moment after your heart beats its last beat and stops. All the people who died in the war aren't dead. All the people who have suffered aren't suffering anymore. They are still alive.

That's the compassion of an infinite perception of negativity— understanding that we don't actually understand. In other words, you might ask yourself, "Why were these children murdered?" or "Why did this earthquake occur?" or "Why are there so many political prisoners in the Third World?" or "Why do we have to suffer pain and evil?" The answers lie in the infinite reasons beyond our finite ego-based perceptions.

So, because this is beyond our understanding, we just have to be compassionate and understand that what people are going through—whether it's a positive event from the ego's point of view, or a negative event—is their evolution.

To grow spiritually, we have to get out of the emotion. That doesn't mean that you aren't going to help people or be a kind person. The idea just detaches you from being flip-flopped around by every political or social event that enhances the ego or detracts from its opinions. What we're looking to do is understand death, pain, cruelty, restriction, discrimination, illness, misfortune, and poverty in a different way—not from a self-obsessed, survivalist attitude of the ego and not from righteous emotions, but from a more distant emotion, one where we understand that there are five billion or more spirits evolving on this physical plane inside physical bodies, and there are certain experiences that these spirits need to pick up as part of this evolution.

Once you understand that, you can step back and take a more angelic stance. Sure, I would prefer that the world didn't experience poverty. I would prefer that the world didn't have wars and strife, pain and agony. I would prefer that there weren't so many military regimes, and restrictions of citizens by their governments. But that's part of this planet's evolution; it's where it finds itself along the time-line of human history.

So we can't go any faster than we're going. We've already evolved enormously. If you take your mind back to, say, a thousand years ago, you'll see how far we've evolved in a millennium. We now have human rights, high-tech medicine, the social contract, our sense of caring. A lot of energy is now being put into conservation and looking after the planet. We've got a long way to go, but we've got to give humanity credit for how far it has come already.

If you get too hung up on the political and social issues, if you get too sucked in to causes, you get very firmly stuck inside the definitions of the ego. This isn't good or bad, necessarily, but if you're trying to embrace the Infinite Self, what you're going to have to do is detach. That's the central part of this philosophy.

Detachment isn't callousness. It's not that you're going to say, "Hey, I don't give a damn about these people." It's just that you have to understand that their evolution is important; it's sacrosanct. Just because a person is in the gutter drunk doesn't mean that he shouldn't be there. One would hope better things for him, but maybe he has to fall to a very low level in order to pick himself up.

Maybe he doesn't want to work himself back up again. Maybe he has a metaphysical need to experience what it feels like to do nothing and degenerate.

So when you see people "doing pain," as I call it, you have to accept that we don't really understand it. So if five people whack a tree, you can get sucked into the energy of it all, or you can say, "Interesting evolutionary experience," remembering they are immortal and not dead.

"Collapse" is the way people learn that they have to change their game plan and raise their energy. We've all been through hard times in our lives. And isn't it true that when you went through a rough patch, there was a moment when you turned it around? You grabbed the bull by the horns and said, "Hey, I'm not going to take this anymore." You started to generate enthusiasm, energy, action, healing, fixing things, looking at yourself and saying, "Wait a minute. I'm a victim of my ego here. I'm going to do something about it."

So when you look at people, you have to look at them from that kind of compassion—from the more distant understanding that we cannot know precisely what people need, metaphysically and spiritually. We don't necessarily understand why things are the way they are. What we can understand is that, given the current state of human evolution, given where people's egos are—where their perception is—this is what's going on. So we'll do our best to spread goodness. But what we won't do is infringe upon people. We won't try to pick them up and fix them if they haven't asked us to.

We have to learn to disengage from the world, for without disengagement we can't journey from ego to spirit because we are locked into the common emotion. I'll talk more about how to escape from that later on.

The point is, are you going to see the world from the insecurity, pompousness, arrogance, dogma, and self-indulgence of the ego's view; or are you going to understand negative energy, misfortune, disease, and death, from the perception of the Infinite Self?

People ask, "How can there be a God if there's so much evil on the earth plane?" The fact is, God isn't involved in the evil. God is detached and just watching it. God isn't saying that there should be evil or that there should be good. God is pure love, existing in the detachment of infinity—watching, and being there for us, but not interfering—allowing each of us to work through what we need to work through.

Certainly, someone can give you a hand up, but in the end, you have to buy your own healing. You either buy it with money because you go to a counselor or practitioner of some kind, or you buy it with energy. Generate more energy, and you heal your life.

Raising people's energy by picking them up from above doesn't work. On an energy level, if you reach down and pick people up, their legs lose contact with the ground. They become disconnected with the reality of where their energy is. They lose sight of what is true and real and feasible—what is do-able today, given their energy.

Now you find that you are responsible for them, and you've got to keep holding them up. God forbid if you ever let them down again and say, "Hey, I helped you for six months, now you're on your own." If you do that, they're going to get extremely pissed off, and they'll tell everyone what a rat you are. You're going to think, "Hang on a minute; that doesn't seem just. I've been helping this guy all this time, and now he's saying what a rat I am." The fact is, you reached down and picked him up. He wasn't necessarily ready. So you infringed upon his evolution by trying to accelerate his perceptions, trying to accelerate his energy without him asking for it. Or perhaps he did ask for it, but you didn't show him how to hold himself up, so eventually he fell back to the energy that is comfortable for him, just like subatomic particles do.

People at my seminars have said to me, "But Stu, you're teaching and helping people raise their energy. Isn't that picking people up and infringing upon them?"

I feel that teaching people is a completely different thing from forcing yourself upon them in a godlike way, changing their evolution and interfering with their life. I don't go knocking on doors saying, "Hey, listen to my lectures, read my books," and so on, offering to underwrite and hold people up for the rest of their lives.

People choose to listen; somebody lends them a book or some coincidence leads them along the path they need. A very nice lady who came to one of my seminars and said the experience changed her life told me that she was there because one day in a bookshop she reached up for a book, and half-a-dozen of my books fell and hit her on the head. She decided it was a message from spirit, and she bought all the books, even though she'd never heard of me and didn't really want them. It must have been a special day. Normally when your name is Wilde you find yourself on the bottom shelf with Zerimski and Zerkofski, in the right-hand, most inaccessible corner of the bookshop, with the dust and the candy wrappers. How my stuff wound up on the top shelf, we'll never know. But it worked for her.

In a previous book, I've told the story of a friend who was thinking about changing her life. She was waiting to cross the road in San Francisco when a car came past and a book fell out of the trunk of the car. That book propelled her life in a new direction.

The Infinite Self has a cute delivery system, which always takes you—sometimes hauls you—to the next stepping stone. You will never see far ahead, but you have to learn to hop from one stone to the next, like a cheery little frog. Then you get up on your hind legs and look for the next stone. Sometimes the way this process works is so delightful, so alluring, I become mesmerized by the graciousness of spirit and the magic of it all.

So remember, when people come to you and ask you for help, do so as best you can. Be kind, be generous, be gracious, be a big person and give of yourself—give of your energy. You don't necessarily have to give of your money, but give of your energy. You can give advice, love, expertise, but don't pick them up. So when they say, "What should I do?" ask "What would you like to do?" "How do I fix this problem?" "How would you like to fix this problem?" "How am I going to get out of this mess?" and "How would you like to get out of this mess?"

You get them to see that the only way up is when they're enthusiastic about their life and their evolution on this earth plane. When their desire to achieve and perceive and create more is greater than the ego's self-indulgence, obstinacy, and destructive ways, then—and only then—will people change.

So, accepting negativity is the concept of, "Hey, we're in an infinite evolution." You're not looking at a group of dead bodies. You're looking at a group of dead bodies whose infinite being has departed and is still alive. There is no death. All the agony we experience emotionally and psychologically is agony of the ego. When you understand that, a big door opens inside you. If the ego didn't have dogma, opinions, and positions it has to defend, you couldn't have negative energy. Somebody would come up to you and say,

"I'm going to shoot you in the head," and you'd say, "Fine, I'm infinite. Do what you need. Meanwhile, I'm going to carry on here, working in my flower garden."

If the ego didn't have rigid opinions, there couldn't be fear. There couldn't be all these people hurting each other. So, understanding negative energy in a different way is important. It's part of people's evolution. If you want to step out of the common emotion, the tribal mind and its predictable emotions, then you're going to have to leave people alone, and you're going to have to understand that that's their evolution, and there's nothing wrong with negativity. We would prefer the world to be perfect, but if it were, we wouldn't be here because we'd have nothing to work on.

Okay, let's continue with these concepts, and we'll chat a bit about human knowledge, belief patterns, strengths, weaknesses, and the masters who walked the earth plane.

STEP 6

WE LEARN ABOUT THE WORLD THROUGH COMMON BELIEF PATTERNS AND THEN GO BEYOND

As I said earlier, what we think we know to be true, we actually borrowed from somebody else. When you were born, your subconscious mind began to record all the sensations and inputs you were exposed to. It also recorded the feelings, emotions, and language it became aware of. But, more importantly, it recorded all the subliminal reactions to the emotions, feelings, and attitudes that were part of your family's day-to-day activities. So bit by bit, you sucked up, without question, the tribal belief patterns you were exposed to.

Those tribal belief patterns aren't likely to contradict the ego, because the central point of the tribe's identity is its ego-self, expressed as the tribal mind. What is a tribe if it isn't just a collection of personalities that come together and belong to one genetic, social, or national group? The tribal mind, by its very nature, is laced with a lot of negativity, fear, and dysfunction. Running through all that is the agenda that the collective ego of the tribe would have you accept.

If you are not very evolved, the tribal mind is a good thing because it offers you the familiarity and safety of a collective consciousness—a collective strength. But once you start to reach for your individuality and your Infinite Self, the tribal mind will bug you. It's too restrictive and controlling to hold you for very long.

On the journey from ego to spirit, you'll want to review and possibly ditch many of those beliefs. Tribal beliefs have their social values, but they also teach fear and restriction. "Don't do this; you'll fail. Don't do that; people won't like it."

For the most part, what the tribe wants you to do is sustain its status quo. The programming that our children receive is one that says, "Put yourself aside, sacrifice yourself for others, and support the tribal good. The tribe needs your energy and support to sustain its power base."

When you incarnated onto this earth plane, the structures and institutions—all the regulations, the whole *modus operandi*, government, taxes, educational system—were already in place. Your Infinite Self had a vision of this and accepted it. At first, you sucked up all the information available. You were trained by your family and teachers at school to be a good little drone and follow the rules. Later in life you could understand all that for what it is.

We tend to think that rules are cast in stone. This is the way it was always done, this is what everybody says, this is how to dress and how to behave. This is hip and cool, and everything else isn't. The human personality desperately needs, as part of its self-image and security, to attempt to elevate itself above others. The tribe does the same. Trying to elevate itself socially over other tribes is part of its security issue. In its need to sustain itself, it requires its members to conform. It doesn't want people being different.

Conformity is dreary because it creates a society of people who are grouped together in a collective globlike evolution. Understand it like this. You're an individual in the sense that you're a unique human within your tribe of origin. But you're not a true spiritual individual until you stand on your own, take charge of your life, and have your own individual destiny, beliefs, and methodology. The tribe won't like you doing that. Our systems are based on control. The whole idea of Congress, government, taxation, the police state, and local controls is designed to milk the taxpayer and impose control. It's illegal to resist, and we are programmed to feel embarrassed or guilty if we push against the status quo. Nowadays, the status quo is not usually benevolent. It tries to perpetuate itself, writing rules to sustain itself.

The attempted imposition of conformity comes from the desire of a nation or a tribe to sustain not only its political and financial identity, but also its psychic integrity. Imagine a couple of thousand years ago when there was little medical knowledge, little real understanding—you can see how the ordinary tribespeople might have been riddled with fear. When a person dropped dead, they couldn't do an autopsy and say, "Yeah, well, he ate a bunch of crud and died of toxic poisoning." They tended to think that misfortunes (what we call contradictions of the ego) such as famine, disease, death, and so on were manifestations of the wrath of God—that God was pissed with the tribe and therefore sent mayhem down upon them. So when the goat died, it was considered a real bad thing. Obviously, the tribesfolk needed food so they were keen on having the use of the goat. Their ignorance put them into a very emotional relationship with their fate and God. So if the crops were good that year, God was pleased. A bad crop, pestilence, disease, another tribe coming down from the hills and kicking them stupid—were all manifestations of the wrath of God.

They didn't know of microbes or bacteria. They didn't have antibiotics. They didn't understand how blood pumps around the body. They had no knowledge. None. Period. Full-stop. So you can understand how they really needed community to feel safe. They needed each other for emotional support and to help defend against attack, to care for the crops, tend the animals, and help raise the kids.

Anybody threatening that psychic collectivism was naturally considered evil, and they had to be banished or put to death. The idea developed that if you didn't believe what the tribe believed, somehow you would make the tribe vulnerable, and God would be displeased because of your lack of faith or action. Maybe you didn't follow through on the great hippopotamus ceremony, or maybe every year in June when they threw two virgins off the cliff, you disagreed with that and said, "I don't fancy this virgin-off-a-cliff routine."

Disagreeing assailed the psychic integrity of the tribe, generating fear. So, even in our modern society where we do have medical knowledge and we understand our physical existence quite well, we still have a sense of duty to conform. If you want to rise up in society, especially within the institutions of the status quo, you are required to fit in, follow the system, and not rock the boat. There is very little opportunity within these institutions and old-style corporations for real creativity.

One of the things that makes me laugh is watching men go to work in the financial district—they're all wearing a funny little piece of colored cloth tied around their necks. Take a long, hard look at it—it's a really weird item of dress, and nobody wonders what it's for. You can't blow your nose with it; that would be considered vulgar. It's not a napkin. What is the purpose of this dangling cloth, often made of silk or colored cotton, tied around the neck?

I don't know if you've noticed, but your neck is where air passes through to the body. You'd think that tying something around your windpipe wouldn't be conducive to your well-being or productivity. Yet millions of men go through the symbolic act of strangling themselves every morning, tying a colored cloth around their windpipe. Weird, man, really weird.

I suppose that originally it was some kind of napkin or serviette that was supposed to stop food from falling down your shirt. But the original meaning has long been lost. Now it serves as a symbol of respectability and reliability. The theory is that crooks and incompetents don't wear ties. Yet nobody in the mainstream has ever put their hand up and said, "Excuse me, what's this thing for?"

If you work in a serious corporation, you're required to strangle yourself with this little piece of cloth. It's a way of joining. If, suddenly, you decide to hang your tie out of your pocket instead of around your neck, or if you decide not to wear it at all, you'd be considered unreliable and a troublemaker.

The whole point of the tribal mind is control. In the olden days, they had to control the women—not just because of psychic integrity, but because the future of the tribe relied on them. The women had to crank out chubbies for the tribe, giving birth to warriors who would defend the joint later on.

So, we've inherited an enormous control of women. It's only recently that women have begun to win equality. Forgive me if this sounds offensive, but in the olden days women were considered the same as cattle. In other words, the more women a tribe had, the more babies they could produce, and therefore the more warriors. Women were a commodity, thought of as part of the wealth of the tribe.

The systems, as a result, needed to control the sexuality of women rigidly. You wouldn't want them banging out chubbies for another tribe. It was only when birth control came along that everything broke down and women could do whatever they wanted. They could raise kids on their own and have sex without worrying about it. They didn't belong to men.

You can see how a lot of the medieval tribal ideas of femininity are still part of our society. There is still the underlying idea that a woman ought to shut up and go and have babies—do what she's supposed to do, not become a millionairess or have any alternative ideas. The tribes controlled through fear, regulations, and punishment. None of that has changed, really.

From protecting the psychic integrity came religious intolerance and control. The tribes weren't keen on anybody forming their own religion. Everyone had to support the integrity of the tribe's communication with God—the ruler of their fate, or so they believed.

If you internalize God, as I asked you to do in Step 1, or as you may have done years ago before you read this book, you'll understand that you don't need a third party to intercede between you and God. If you want to talk to God, all you have to do is quiet the mind through meditation and contemplation and chat away.

In the olden days, the idea was that individuals were too weak and sinful to have a meaningful dialogue with God. So, systems were developed whereby people had to use a third party to communicate with God. Once you had a third party, then all the rules, guilt, and obligations came into play. Now we have a system where there are millions of people on the earth plane who believe that the God Force is within them and they are spiritually free, while others still believe that they are weak and that God is outside of them, so they need someone to intercede on their behalf.

It doesn't mean that you can't be part of a church if you want to be. But control is a very old-fashioned idea, so it had better be a liberal church. Some people enjoy the camaraderie, the friendship, the music, the hymns and the hers, they like being taught by a knowledgeable holy man or woman. Fair enough—if that's what you're into. But the thing to remember is that most of these systems are not designed to set you free.

I was attracted to the philosophy of Taoism because it is not a church—it's an idea to liberate you from pain. Nice one! Taoism doesn't impose any guilt trips on you or make you pay ten percent of your money or load you up with a sack full of do's and don'ts.

It's not to say that all tribal ideas were silly. Some of them made sense. They were ideas about health and hygiene, how to grow food, and how to interrelate peacefully with other members of the tribe. But a lot of it had to do with conforming, control, and making sure you didn't rise above the pack, or woe is you—leave the tribe.

So, we come onto the earth plane and we accept the tribal belief patterns as being what they are—they will gradually change over the course of time. As you grow more self-confident and become spiritually mature, you'll soon reach a point where you can release most of the tribal ideas without too much apprehension and fear. Then you are free to become an individual, a true spiritual being with a spiritual destiny of your own.

To do that, you have to go beyond the discomfort of distancing yourself from the tribal beliefs, which usually also means you'll disconnect yourself from its acceptance and support. Once you are strong enough and have the confidence to stand on your own, you'll become a real individual—you'll believe in yourself so strongly that you can be different and not worry what others think.

One of the exercises I gave people in a seminar once was to put on a chicken outfit and go to work. So throw away the little piece of cloth around your neck, and put on a chicken outfit instead. Don't explain to anybody at the office why you're wearing a chicken outfit. Let's say you work in a bank. Just walk in, sit down, and start cashing people's checks. When your co-workers ask, "Why are you wearing a chicken outfit?" answer "What chicken outfit?" The point of this exercise is for you to get into the habit of believing in yourself as a solid inner identity, a spirit, rather than a social projection of self, who has to fit in and win approval by saying all the right things and wearing all the socially acceptable uniforms. Instead, you can say to yourself, "I am what I am. I'm a divine spirit inside a body that happens to be wearing a chicken outfit."

In one seminar, I had three guys from an Australian army commando unit. They really took this idea to heart and marched off to their military barracks dressed in ballerinas' tutu dresses. When they walked past the guard at the gate, he saluted them! You've got to give those lads credit for really believing in themselves—for saying, "I am what I am. I don't have to conform to keep you happy."

A lot of those conformity issues stem from childhood, and the need of the ego to seek the approval of others. The object of conforming is to keep others happy and to feel accepted. "If I do this and that, will you love me?" "If I have sex with you whenever you want me to, will you love me?" "If I say these nice things, will you consider me holy or spiritual?"

Of course, conformity is imposed from above as a control mechanism. Mostly it's imposed from within, as you'll be afraid initially of breaking out of the status quo—in case you're banished, criticized, or judged. If you've never broken out of the status quo, then tomorrow do something nice and crazy. Go to work in your swimming trunks. Don't put the tie on; wrap your mother's scarf round your neck instead. Spend all day walking backwards. When people ask, "Why are you walking backwards?" say "I like to know where I've been."

Do things to break up the binding rigidity that the mind imposes on you, and the fear it has of breaking away from the mold. Remember, if you can't break away, you're spiritually stuck—forever and ever, amen. You'll have to trot along in the collective destiny of your people. You can't create an alternative reality and a truly independent spiritual evolution for yourself until you break away a little.

For the next two weeks, invent half a dozen ways to break up your normal rhythm of life. For example, go to a restaurant and order your dinner backwards. Start with the coffee, go to the ice cream, then the main dish, and finish with the starter. Pick types of food you never eat. If you hate jazz, go to a jazz club; if you hate broccoli, order a bunch of it at every meal for a week. The routine you are familiar with day-to-day is part of your ego's authority over you. By doing things differently, you begin to challenge its authority.

STEP 7

ALL HUMAN KNOWLEDGE IS
AFFECTED BY HUMAN WEAKNESS

Weakness is endemic to our human situation. Most of the weaknesses are various manifestations of the ego's fear of death. I'm going to talk about death later on, but this idea of sustaining—saving, holding on, restricting, being careful, not taking any risks—comes from the ego's fear and uneasiness because it's unsure that things will last or what will happen next. It's part of our mortality. We have all those weaknesses inside us, not just the fear that the ego experiences, but also the emotional self-indulgence it puts us through.

One of the things that will start to bug you as you trot along the spiritual path is the enormous self-indulgence we all labor under. The ego is grim when it comes to indulging itself in silliness. It tells itself terrible lies. It constantly seeks to make itself important. It wants things for nothing. It wants reassurance. It needs attention. It is always seeking to gratify itself.

It's not surprising that we become victims of the ego. The ego feels insecure, so it's constantly trying to ameliorate that insecurity, looking for experiences or things that will make it feel better. But everything you do to keep the ego happy only serves as a temporary respite. You can't control the ego by keeping it happy; you can only win back control of your life via discipline and going beyond the ego's inherent weakness.

And, of course, a lot of that weakness comes from the ego's sense of not knowing, which causes a terrible disquiet. However, as you embrace the spiritual path, you'll understand that you're in flow. You're only going to see a few yards in front of you. Everything becomes beautifully spontaneous. Nothing is laid out in little rows anymore.

So, one of the ideas to remember is that the need to feel secure is only a bad habit. You can feel secure even when you don't know what will happen next. It's only a custom of ego that requires you to "need to know." You don't! When you become more infinite in your perception, you become more open, and knowing what will happen next becomes less important. It's the difference between flow and restriction. You can be quite secure even when you don't know. When people say to you, "What do you know?" you can say, "Nothing. I don't know, don't care." Then you transcend the weakness of the ego so that it is reluctant to move. You're going to have to move without knowing, just feeling your way along and asking yourself constantly, "Hey, how does this feel? Does it feel right?" If it doesn't, make adjustments.

When you can come to "Don't know, don't care," you're free. Instantly you go past one of the great human weaknesses—the need to know. If you're balanced today, you'll be more balanced tomorrow because your energy is rising constantly. If you're abundant today, you'll be more abundant tomorrow because that is how rising energy works. Once you comprehend the nature of the weakness of this existence, it becomes a huge triumph and a great thrill to go beyond that weakness. In the end, that's what this journey is all about.

In my view, self-indulgence is one of the major weaknesses we have to contend with; it blocks our spiritual development, and it's arrogant. The idea that somebody owes you a living, somebody owes you importance, somebody owes you respect, somebody owes you an opportunity—it's silly. To become an infinite being, you're going to have to be self-sufficient. So if you believe that somebody out there is going to provide for you, you can't dominate your journey through this physical plane.

You have to prove your mastery of this physical dimension by generating enough energy to sustain yourself. If you can't earn loads of money now, begin by reducing your needs. Saying, "I've got to have this, I've got to have that," is self-indulgent and destructive because it affirms your lack. What you ought to say instead is "I have less money so I'm going to consume less. Maybe I'll live in a cheaper dwelling, get a cheaper car, eat less, spend less money on beer."

People naturally think that the way to solve their money problems is to earn more money. Of course that helps, but the real answer lies in discipline and balance. If your ego is out of control at, say, the level of $1,000 per month, you'll be in even more trouble at $2,000 a month. And if you suddenly earned $10,000 and you had the same lack of discipline, you'd soon be in serious financial trouble. In fact, the more you earn, the more trouble you'll get yourself into. So the Infinite Self protects you from your own imbalance. It makes quite sure you don't get yourself into too much trouble by earning too much money.

The way to expand your wealth and get on top of things is to cut out the nonvital ego expenses and to discipline yourself to stay inside whatever money you do have. I've talked a lot about the metaphysics of money elsewhere in my writings, but the main secret to abundance comes from the emotional balance and stability you project when you are in control. If you are harassed or worried about money, the insecurity you emit goes out to others as an insecure subliminal signal. It destroys your ability to earn more.

The secret to having enormous amounts of wealth is to not need it. Then it comes to you naturally. When you are desperate and you are trying to force things to happen, money hops up the road in front of you, tantalizingly just out of reach most of the time. So the trick is to spend less than you earn. Then you can make more and more money and get as rich as you like, and you'll never have problems.

In addition, I think it's important to remember that on the spiritual path, there are no guarantees. It's futile to seek one. The only exception is energy. If you have energy, that's your guarantee. If you don't have energy, you'll become imbalanced—things will start coming at you. Simple, really.

From self-indulgence comes self-importance. Don't get into status trips: where you are in the pecking order, who's up and who's down, who's hip and who isn't, who's spiritual and who isn't spiritual. All of that is just snobbery.

When you look at our world full of conceit, pomposity, and arrogance—everyone jostling, posing, seeking attention—all that Hollywood glamour stuff—it's grim. It's a lot of weakness and hype, seeking to be heard, competing to promote itself, desperate to make itself special. The Tao says:

> *To be always talking is against nature...he who boasts*
> *of what he will do succeeds in nothing...That is why he*
> *that possesses Tao does not linger.*

Because the initiate is strong, he or she doesn't care to linger around, waiting for praise or attention. These people don't need to be considered special. The initiate is happy to stand at the back, to take the lowest place, to be silent. The Taoists revered water because they saw it as a symbol of humility and service. Water nurtures and sustains all living things, and yet it seeks nothing for itself—it always flows to the lowest spot.

So, be like water, be humble, nurture yourself and others. And stay at the back, where you are free to slip in and out of life's situations unnoticed and unencumbered. That is the watercourse way.

You don't need razzmatazz and glamour. That only serves to create emotional weight in your life, pumping the ego into a false sense of importance. Too much hype and attention, and the ego becomes a spoiled brat and impossible to control. It will soon drag you away from the Tao, from what is natural and good. Trash that nonsense before it makes you sick. You don't need it. All you need is balance—and the contentment, creativity, love, and comprehension that flows from that. And from these beautiful things you will understand your spiritual place. And from that flows silent power, gratitude, and sacredness. These are the real things; everything else is maya, hype, and *BS*. It won't last.

What people yearn for makes them weak. When you fall in love and yearn for another person, the very fact that you are desperate for him or her weakens you. It often means you can't have this person. Your stifling need makes the other person uncomfortable, and they back away. When you yearn for a particular goal in life—leaning toward it emotionally, pushing for it—you affirm that you don't have it. Thus, you push the very thing you want away from yourself.

So, control that yearning. Say, "Hey, I'd like to have a new car, but I can't afford it at this time. I feel abundant; I feel the car is becoming a part of my life. I'll get it later, or perhaps something even better will come along." Then work in a concerted way toward materializing your goal. Don't yearn and don't moan. Take a moment each day before you go to sleep or before you rise in the morning to give thanks for what you *do* have. "This life is beautiful. These children are beautiful. This home isn't so great, but thank you, thank you, Great Spirit, for providing a shelter. Thank you for these clothes and these friendships. Thank you for these economic opportunities."

The other human weakness is guilt. Guilt is self-indulgence that comes from remorse, and it has been successfully used by society as a control mechanism. If you don't follow along, people judge you as a rotten person. The fact is, most of the things you might feel guilty about are just rules other people created.

In the eternal Tao, there are no ups and downs; there is no good and evil. There is high energy that sets people free and expresses love, and there's low energy that restricts, controls, and manipulates people. But it is only energy. There are no absolutes and no judgments in the grace of the Infinite Self.

I don't believe, in the strict metaphysical sense, that there are any completely innocent victims. If you put out thought-forms of restriction, weakness, manipulation, and lack, you pull to you negative experiences. In the totality of an infinite perception, the victim and the aggressor are one and the same energy. If you have done something wrong to somebody, yes, you could have chosen a more righteous way of acting. But on the other hand, they put out negative energy and as a result pulled you into their life. You messed them up at your own time and expense. They can say, "Thank you, God, for sending me a teacher who has messed me up and infringed upon me. It taught me things."

Guilt is a worthless energy. If you've messed up or failed, grant yourself absolution. Then draw a line in the sand and say, "From now on, I'm going to act in a better way. I'm going to act in a more honorable way." The important thing is to truncate the emotion of that guilt before it becomes overwhelming. Forgive yourself, and realize that in the eternal spiritual sense, there isn't any real sin; there is only forgiveness. Yes, there are low-energy actions that infringe and restrict, and there are high-energy actions that love, liberate, inspire, and release people. But that's all there is. We come to experience both types of action in this lifetime.

Naturally, as a spiritual person working on yourself, you're going to try to choose as many high-energy, liberating attitudes and actions as you can. But if sometimes you go the other way and fail, you haven't really failed. All you've done is gone up the other end of the scale. You have to understand contrast in order to learn. Bit by bit, you will strengthen, become more, and learn a better way. Sometimes you may have to fall apart or do something that is really infringing on others—because that's what you needed at the time, and that's what you did. So you can absolve yourself and move on.

The other weakness that affects people is a poor self-image, which invariably comes from childhood experiences and the parenting you received. Everything is fixable. You can work on self-image without necessarily healing all your inner-child wounds if you will concentrate and love yourself, and if you will set aside quiet time and do inner work, acknowledging yourself for the things you have achieved. If you try to improve yourself, raise your energy, exercise more, and become more organized, bit by bit the self-image starts to build.

The whole point of the journey from ego to spirit is one of acceptance. If you aren't very confident or have a poor self-image, the first thing you need to do is accept that. The second thing is to gradually go past your shame, past your guilt, and work your way to where you can look at yourself in the mirror and say, "Hey, this person is okay. We're moving up." The weakness of self-image is part of your experience and programming. You are here to transcend it. It forms a pivotal part of your sacred quest. So be brave and don't be victimized by your inadequacies. They are just your teachers. They will strengthen you as you overcome them, and you will forge a new spiritual vision for yourself.

To recapitulate: don't bitch about your weaknesses; either work on them or ignore them, and concentrate on your strengths instead. If you do so, usually your weaknesses will fall away and become less dominant in your life.

There's an enormous power inside you. It is the infinite power that flows from your connection to the God Force. You have the power if you will accept an infinite perception and if you start to see yourself in that way.

This brings me to the next step, which is to realize that the masters who walked this planet in ancient history were masters primarily because the people who surrounded them at that time were uneducated and psychologically and metaphysically weak.

STEP 8

THE MASTERS
WERE SUPERNATURAL
BECAUSE OTHERS WERE NOT

Go back several thousand years to the time when the tribes were ignorant. Suddenly an immense energy such as Jesus or Buddha pops up—an energy so far ahead of the little people. It's not surprising that they made these masters into gods. It had to be. They would naturally look up to and deify anyone who had even a modicum of perception and understanding.

The Christ consciousness, the Buddhahood, the flow of energy these masters tapped into, is available today. It isn't something that has disappeared. People will tell you that the only way to access the power is through this philosophy or that spiritual group. But, in fact, the energy of the masters is here today—and even more so than back then.

Extrasensory perception, ancient wisdoms, miracles, and all manner of heightened awareness and phenomena are still available. Energy does not disappear; it just changes. In this case, it has risen as our comprehension and our belief in self has expanded.

In 500 B.C., when Lao-Tzu sat under his little tree and wrote the Tao Te Ching, he could have had electricity to light his paper. The electricity was always here. All of the energies have always been here and always will be here. Okay, it took us another two-and-a-half thousand years to discover it and harness it, but the energy of the Christ consciousness, the energy of the masters, is perpetual. If, in your prayers and meditations, you start to call upon that energy, upon the name of your teacher, the name of your god, or upon the God Force within you, you begin to tap that power. It doesn't know you want it until you tell it—just as electricity didn't know humans needed it, so it lay dormant here since the beginning of the earth.

We haven't begun to really comprehend what a human is capable of. In addition, we are limited by beliefs that are many thousands of years old. We have to dream a few impossible dreams and then multiply that by several million, and then begin to dream an enormous dream. We are still way behind the times.

Most of our metaphysical, spiritual, and religious beliefs originated at least 2,000 years ago. Whereas we've advanced tremendously in technology, science, medicine, biology, and chemistry, our metaphysical knowledge is still Neanderthal.

You have the same amount of power that the masters had. You can sit in a meditation and visualize in the same way that Jesus, Buddha Lao-Tzu, or Mohammed did. You can feel beyond today's knowledge, to knowledge that isn't normally available. You can touch into what the Theosophists call the *Akashic Record*—which is best described as the "collective unconscious" wherein is stored all the knowledge our humanity has ever had. You can align to that and add a few hitherto undiscovered ideas from your own imagination and experimentation.

If you're learning to play the guitar, listen to the best guitar player who has ever been. Put yourself into the mind and feeling of that guitar player. Become him or her as you learn to play. If you want to be a great football player, watch the reruns of the greatest athletes who ever played the game, and enter the vibrancy and enthusiasm of their energy. It's all still there—the genius of Einstein, Beethoven, Mozart, Isaac Newton, Edison, Tesla—all that knowledge and energy is available right now.

Rather than looking at the masters as something on a pedestal that you can never reach, you can internalize and utilize the masters' energy. Internalize the Christ consciousness, the Buddhahood, that Light. Then make yourself a part of it. Align to where there's brilliance. Align to the power of miracles, and feel it inside of you. If Jesus could put his hand upon people and heal them, so can you.

That is the exciting part of the spirituality within—tapping into all the inspiration, wisdom, and knowledge that has been forgotten, recreating it, and then offering it to others.

Come with me now to the next section, and we'll talk a little bit about how discipline helps to center the mind—how you will consolidate and double your power as quickly as possible. Come, let's have a little chat about that.

STEP 9

POWER COMES FROM DISCIPLINE

I was 28 years old when I first got into an understanding of the Tao and the Infinite Self. What drove me more than anything else was the desire to comprehend the unseen worlds around us and the true nature of our potential as humans.

I remember one day, driving through Putney in London, there was a small church on the main drag, and I parked my car and went in. I didn't know why. The church was almost empty. I knelt down at the back of the church and looked around. It was old and beautiful, as many Victorian churches are; there was an organist practicing above me in the choir gallery—Bach's *Fugue*, as I recall.

I remember saying to myself, "Who am I? What do I want in this lifetime? What are my goals?" I pondered for a moment and realized that what I really wanted was knowledge. So I put my arms out, looked up in the vague direction of the heavens, and said, "God, make me truly wise. Give me wisdom." I didn't ask for glamour, power, enormous amounts of money, or an easy life. I asked for wisdom.

That was one of the most impacting days of my life, because that stated desire for wisdom became my affirmation in this lifetime. It wasn't long after that I met a guy who was teaching a special theta brainwave meditation course, a course in the art of deep trance. Having met him, I soon met other teachers and went on from there. Bit by bit, I did get a certain amount of wisdom, and I'm still getting it. So the God Force is still supplying on the deal I made with it in that little church in Putney many years ago, and bless its little cotton socks!

I suppose that when it comes to the crunch, is your desire for wisdom greater than your need to accommodate the ego? In your tussle with the ego, to decide who will control your life, you must have a certain amount of self-discipline, or the ego will always win. So Step 9 is the realization that real power comes from discipline. True power, true knowledge—the ability to embrace the Infinite Self and transcend this physical plane and peer into other worlds, other perceptions—comes only from discipline. Why?

It's not as if God is sitting up there somewhere—bless It—saying, "You've got to do this, and I want you to do that." God is an energy. It does not react emotionally and It's not bothered whether you get yourself together or not. No, discipline is important because without it you can't control the mind. If you can't control yourself, you are always a victim of the brat within; instead of becoming a spiritual grown-up, you remain, in the spiritual sense, an adolescent.

So you have to start making yourself do things that help you exert control. Mention discipline and most people flee, like the Mongols are just about to come down off the hills. It's comical, the gyrations the ego will go through rather than accept your authority over it. I think it's best to creep up on it gradually. Invent things, one after the next—some disciplines of a minor nature, others more major, but get the ego used to the idea that you are going to get it doing things it doesn't necessarily like. It's got to buy the idea that you are in control. For the most part, it doesn't matter what disciplines you pick as long as you pick something.

Here are a few that worked for me. The first is the discipline of serenity. Most don't see serenity as a discipline, but in a modern world you have to work hard to enforce stillness and quiet time on your own. Activity feeds the personality with gratification, and it makes the ego feel important. Quiet time, serenity, and silence disempower the ego and make the inner you more special. It's a nice balance. So turn off the TV, unplug the phone, play soft, ambient music, or remain in silence for an hour or two. If you can't manage that long because you really are too busy, at least try to manage ten or fifteen minutes each day. Stillness and quiet are the way you pray to the inner self.

As a part of your overall serenity, it's important to try to disengage from arguments and all the antagonistic, adversarial positions you may find yourself in. It's hard to go beyond tick-tock and embrace a more angelic way if you're constantly at war with people. In the act of scrapping with others, you metaphysically hold yourself back. Your energy can't rise while you're busy arguing with the Neanderthals in the marketplace of life. It doesn't matter if your cause is just or unjust; it's the emotion and thought-forms of an argument that lock you in. Sometimes arguments are unavoidable, especially if you have a lot of social and financial interactions going on in your life. Sooner or later a few plates fall off the shelf, so to speak. But keep your disputes short and as unemotional as possible. If you have any outstanding situations with people, try to resolve them.

You don't have to fall in love with everybody, but at least try to reconcile the situation as best as possible so the emotion of it doesn't control you. Get rid of the troublemakers even if it costs you a little or if it forces you to back down; wish them well and send them on their way. Freedom is more important than winning turf wars for the ego.

Another discipline I have found particularly important is to establish order in your life. Messy surroundings and an untidy life reflect a weakened metaphysical and psychological state. If you are powerful, you will dominate your life, you will find time to clean up and order things, and you will want to do that as a part of your personal discipline. Mess is the external manifestation of the ego's disquiet and laziness. Through mess, the ego exercises control over you. It's the brat within—obsessed with self, waiting for its mother to pick up after it. Or, sometimes, the brat from hell is just too important and special and full of itself to do mundane stuff like cleaning up and washing dishes. All the more reason to give it a whole pile of stuff to polish and clean. The more you accommodate the brat, the more it will make your life a misery.

Make your life as immaculate as possible, and keep things *zen* and neat. Order helps you feel confident. Life becomes a prayer rather than the chaotic manifesto of an immature mind. The effort it takes to establish order is recouped in several ways. As an affirmation of control, it helps you feel more secure. It allows for a better flow of ideas and, most importantly, you don't waste energy hunting for things, stepping over a dead horse in the hallway every time the doorbell goes.

There are many simple and powerful disciplines you can invent for yourself. It's mostly doing things that help you, rather than gratifying the ego. Try the discipline of rising early, taking cold showers, walking in the park or woods before dawn. The ancients saw the grace of God in the simplicity and humility and abundance of nature: the animals, the wind, the water, the warmth of the sun, and through the ebb and flow of the ever-changing seasons. I walked in the forest every night for three years. I learned to become friends with the rain and the snow, and discovered how to keep warm just using my mind. I went beyond my fears of the dark.

On beautiful nights, I'd lie on a large rock looking upwards at the starlit sky. I'd call on the Immense Goodness to show me things I didn't know already. I was always there, every night, bugging it, walking in silence, digging deep inside myself to discover things. The God Force is cool. It shows you things. Some of the stuff It has shown me, I never did understand, but that isn't Its fault.

Sometimes the weather was atrocious. But I walked, nonetheless; it was my discipline. I learned to ignore the weather. I wasn't going to let my personality whine and moan because it was windy or hailing or cold or snowing or whatever. I was going to "do" weather, and not react.

I learned a special kind of walking—a way of stepping that comes from one of the monastic orders in China. I think it's called "tiger walking." Rather than putting your heel down first then your toes as we normally do when walking, in the tiger walk you point your foot forward with each step, placing the outside of the foot down first, then the toes and finally the heel.

I don't know if you remember the old TV show, *Kung Fu,* but there was a scene in the intro when "little grasshopper" had to walk on rice paper while the head dude (the one with ping-pong balls for eyes) stood by. Well, tiger walking is a bit like the same step. It's very graceful and silent, but it's not easy to do. It forces you to concentrate while you're walking. I would "do" my tiger walking for an hour or so, then I'd come home and "do" having a cup of tea, and I'd complete my morning discipline with a 24-minute meditation. That's my preferred method—one minute of meditation for each hour of the day.

In the early days, I used a theta metronome for meditation; this emits a clicking sound that oscillates at four to six cycles per second. Your brain cells start to lock into metronomic rhythm, and you enter a low-brain speed, a trancelike state, without any real effort or previous experience. You can buy electronic gizmos that generate a variety of meditation sounds, but they tend to be expensive. A regular theta audio tape is cheaper; loads of companies sell them.

The point about walking and meditating is that in using your will to enforce stillness, you disempower the ego's dominance. It's important to become self-disciplined, inventing ways to challenge or control one's personality. It puts you in the driver's seat, assisting you to detach from negative emotion. Among the disciplines I took on was vegetarianism, which I did for seven years. I did the walking for three years. I've meditated pretty much every day since the beginning of my spiritual journey.

I've also taken time out each day to review the day. This process comes from the Hindu tradition and is usually done at night. It involves reviewing the day's events, in the mind's eye, running backwards through the day from bedtime to dawn. Don't ponder or comment too much on what happened—just watch. This exercise is a way of unraveling those experiences. It cuts down on the need for lots of trivial dreams, where the mind processes things that happened during the day. It's like moving backwards in time; it's a discipline to do just as you fall asleep so that you notice your life. Life will not be just passing you by; you're taking time to notice it. In reviewing the day's events, it unclutters the mind and allows you to go to sleep in a very pure state of consciousness. Much of the inner communication you have with the all-knowing of Infinite Self is initially at night.

If you have a particular problem on your mind, put it up for review during the night. Ask your Infinite Self to consider it. Say, "Tonight I want to review this particular situation. Please provide the answer to my problem by the morning." Next day, either when you wake or later on, ideas and solutions will drift into your mind. Doing the process allows you to establish a more solid communication between your intellectual-emotional self, which is doing the day-to-day living, and the Infinite Self within that is the real you.

Another discipline, which I'll mention in detail in Step 14, is the discipline of not criticizing and judging. Just like arguing and fighting, criticizing and judging lock you into the ego's world, denying you access to the infinite world. Through serenity, you disengage from disturbance of the tribal emotions, and it helps you detach from your own emotions. Make time to be on your own, time to really contemplate who you are. It's a marvelous experience if you haven't done it. You start to figure out, Who is this person?

Try this: find a dark room, light a candle, and sit in front of a mirror. Stare at yourself, looking slightly downward—it's more restful for your eyes. Stare at the center of your being in the area of your heart. Just watch in silence as you stare at your image reflected there. Blink as little as possible, and do this for half an hour. You may start to see your reflection change; various faces may appear superimposed over yours as your innermost feelings begin to come at you from out of the mirror. You will have new perceptions, and if you use the metronome as suggested, it will help you induce the theta trance state. Visions come to mind, and sometimes other worlds open to give you a glimpse of celestial dimensions. Sometimes it will seem like those other worlds are reaching out for you from the mirror. Just watch; don't let them freak you out. You'll soon get used to it.

The mirror exercise, silent walking, and meditation begin to show you the true multidimensional nature of this physical reality. As you embrace the Infinite Self, it will show you things that you have never seen before. Sometimes they are simple things like the spaces between the leaves of a tree or the silence between words in conversations. Sometimes it shows you major stuff, like the doorway between two worlds; suddenly you see the twilight nonworld hovering between the in-breathing and the out-breathing of this cosmic experience we call life. Your inner and outer selves enter into a delightful conversation and soon melt into one, and the outer reality changes to reflect the serenity of the inner you.

You will ask a question of yourself, and a bus will pass with an advertisement for shampoo pasted on its side, and the text of the ad will answer your question. Life becomes a symbol of the inner you, a part of that dynamic interactive dialogue with everything around you. The Infinite Self is there to guide and teach you, to lead you on to more and more energy. But discipline is vital, because you cannot begin to wrestle the ego into submission without discipline.

STEP 10

CENTERING THE MIND

Centering the mind is vital in the discovery of self. Without mental discipline and control, life's a losing battle. It's like having 40 chickens in a truck and they're constantly flying about. There are feathers everywhere, and a tremendous commotion is going on. Somehow you've got to sit your chickens down in little rows and keep them quiet.

Centering the mind is a discipline you perform in the waking state as well as the meditative state. In the waking state, it's mostly a matter of training yourself to observe life rather than react to it. The mind, perceiving through the five senses, is programmed to react. So, somebody says something and the untamed mind responds, sometimes obviously, sometimes more subtly—anger, happiness, joy, frustration, whatever.

What you're looking to do as a part of centering yourself is to complete the process of detachment by training yourself not to react. You need distance, not involvement; action, not reaction. You have to buy the solution in life, not the emotion. Learn to become an observer of life and an observer of self.

The classic example that I use in my lectures is the way people react to being in the rain. Rain is a teacher. It's perfect for learning detachment. People don't like rain; they react negatively, often becoming angry and dysfunctional. It's comical watching them go through their prissy routines while trying to dodge raindrops. You can react and go through all that stupidity, or you can just agree to "do" rain. Next time it's absolutely pelting down, get your best clothes and coat on, and maybe invest in a fancy hairdo and, just as it starts to really come down, get out there. Have no resistance to the cold. Experience the wet, "do" cold, experience slush, just say, "Hey, I'm doing rain here." Rain is normal; it's a gift. You're walking along eternal, immortal, and infinite, and it's pissin' down. So what?

Practice doing rain, then you can do "dinner with the mother-in-law" or "talking to the bank manager about the state of your account" or anything else that makes you uneasy. So if the car is not in the parking lot when you get out there next time, just agree to do "no car," and say, "Oh, I'm tiger walking now, as my car has gone."

The people you meet regularly—friends and relatives, work-mates who bug you, people who are particularly awkward to deal with—let them be your teachers. When they make you uncomfortable and drive you crazy, use that as a test of your composure and strength. Step back and watch; don't react. Bit by bit you'll see how, perhaps, you've let others exert control over you in the past because they knew they could trigger your negative reaction. When you don't react, you are free; you'll get a clearer perception of how best to handle difficult interpersonal situations. Perhaps what you need is to do "airport." As I said in one of my other books, airports are one of the truly great modern inventions. I'm a great believer in airports—there's not much you can't heal with a little bit of "airport."

Become a silent observer of life and a compassionate observer of yourself. You are not your emotions or your body or your personality and its ego. These are only a part of what you are. In fact, you're a divine energy that is evolving, operating through the complexities of body, mind, and emotions to comprehend itself as a spiritual angel, an eternal spirit that is growing and learning, poised in infinity and currently doing "human being."

Now let's go back to the obvious part of centering the mind, which takes us back, of course, to the meditative state. I can't see how you can reach that infinity within you without contemplation and meditation. Somehow you have to access the subconscious mind, where all your deeper impulses and urges are. If you don't look at the subconscious mind and observe the social and intellectual programming you received, you'll never see why things are the way they are and how the innermost complexity of your feelings project out into your life. You'll never properly understand how these various factors have resulted in the circumstances of your life. Without contemplation and looking within, you are flying blind; you have no real way to understand who you are.

Most people's experience of life on the planet is just external. They observe the results of their actions solely from the ego's opinion and viewpoint. It is a life of confusion and pain, and it is often rather sad. They become victims of their minds. They blame others when, in fact, the answer lies in their subliminal urges, desires, impulses, and fears.

They try to heal themselves by attempting to eliminate their reactions: "I'm scared, I'd better do something—eat chocolate, drink, take some drugs—anything to stop the nasty feeling I'm experiencing." But you know you can't heal yourself by giving your fears and reactions chocolate. One day you have to discover where in your programming the fears come from, and then you can eliminate them.

"Why is it that when I see a man with a green coat and umbrella, I get scared?" you ask. Because when you were five, a man in a green coat carrying an umbrella went "boo" and frightened you. And even though you may not even remember the event, you are now trained to react to guys in green.

All of the puzzles of life have an answer in the subconscious mind. It takes a while to reach in there and pick it all out, but the process of looking within unravels the knots and complications that have built up over the years.

Meditation need not be complicated. Some will tell you that nothing less than sitting cross-legged in the lotus position, *ohm*'ing yer ohms in the temple, will do. In fact, any meditation which is painful or uncomfortable to perform is distracting in my view. Okay, so you've got your robes on and you can stick your toe in your ear, big deal. When you think about it practically, how many times are you going to really need to clean your ear with your toe in this lifetime? Excuse me! What's it for?

Anyway, there you are, all contorted, and everyone can see how incredibly spiritual you are. And you're sitting there as pleased as punch—mega holy-moly while the God Force slips away quietly to throw up. Any time you have to put on a performance so people can see your spirituality, you've lost the plot. The ego has tricked you. The performance in itself says you don't really believe. The Infinite Self is invisible. Any ol' meditation style is just fine; it doesn't have to be a great performance unless you really want it that way.

In a way, meditation is quite a cerebral process because it is the art of thinking about not thinking. It doesn't suit many people, especially women, who often come so much from their feelings that they find they just can't meditate in the traditional way. So each should meditate in their own way, in whatever way feels comfortable—during a massage or body work, while playing with your children, or during some contemplative activity. All that is fine; I don't think there is any one way, no right and wrong.

As part of this discussion on meditation, let's talk briefly about brain waves. In the waking state, your brain is oscillating at approximately 14 cycles a second and above. That doesn't mean your whole brain is oscillating at that speed; it means that it is predominantly at that wave band. It's known as the beta state; it's the normal waking state.

Down from that is the slower alpha state. A lot is known about alpha. There are loads of books you can read and courses you can take to learn to generate alpha. It is a light meditative state, the wave band of intuition and some ESP. It's also where dreams seem to take place. You're in alpha when the brain oscillates at between seven and fourteen cycles a second. It's very regenerative—great for stress reduction, light meditation, and just allowing you to enjoy physiological relaxation.

Below the alpha state is the theta wave band, which is four to six cycles per second. Theta is the trance state. When your brain is firing theta, you'll be able to feel your physical body, but only minimally. In theta you drift out of the ego's perception, and you become universal mind. What I found so fascinating about the theta state is that it doesn't take very long to learn how to generate it, especially if you use the metronome as discussed.

Triggering the theta state is an excellent discipline, because as you go into deep meditation, what you're really doing is disempowering the ego. You're telling the personality, "Listen, sit down and shut up." Sure, at the beginning it's going to come up with little thought-forms such as, "Hey, we need to service the car" and that kind of stuff. But you begin to push against the thoughts that come in there. You say, "I don't accept that energy; I'll handle the car later. I don't accept that perception; I'm changing my views. Thank you very much for telling me about this fear, but I don't accept that fear as a reality in my life. When and if I need to act, I will."

As you start to push against the thoughts that come up and you begin to control the flow of activity from the mind, you'll start to reach for that place deep within you that is holy and spiritual—the place where you enter into the embrace of the Infinite Self. Soon you'll see that you are not just your own mind, but a part of the molecule that makes up the global mind. Beyond the molecule of the global mind is the molecule that makes up the cosmic mind, which would be the mind of God, the mind of everything that exists—past, present, and future. Click—a door opens, and you enter into your rightful place. It's a magical world.

Meditation also begins to change you physiologically. The chemical make-up of the brain is a by-product of your moods, feelings, and attitudes. That's only been discovered in the last ten years. Initially, moods and attitudes were thought to be a by-product of the brain's chemical cocktail, but it is now widely known that, in fact, we alter the cocktail in the brain through how we feel.

The chemicals in your brain react to emotion. So, a person who is neurotic or hysterical will gradually change the chemical mix in the brain, and he or she will become more hysterical. If you're slightly psychotic and you allow yourself to wander around like that for a period of time, the cocktail of chemicals in your brain changes to reflect your mood. Similarly, if you are very negative, the cocktail changes and you become more negative.

If you start to enter your rightful serenity, your spiritual home, the cocktail in your brain starts to become more serene. The endorphins begin to fire, you become happier, serotonin levels change, and calmness descends upon you. All of a sudden you begin to create a complete and settled person—by changing the physiological nature of the brain.

By taking on a meditative discipline, and by doing it for 24 minutes a day, you'll begin to affirm, "I am in control. I am establishing control over myself, my emotions, my ideas, and intellect. I, not my ego, am in charge of my life." What you're actually saying is, "I'm not my personality. Sure, I have to operate through my personality, but I'm not only my personality and its desires and reactions. I am an infinite being observing my personality."

So, find a comfy spot to meditate—preferably in the morning before the rest of the world has gotten up—and play your metronome and sit. In the beginning it will be a bit frustrating because you'll experience nothing in particular. But little by little, you're going to see colored blobs in front of your eyes. Let them pass.

Then symbols will come to you. You'll peer into what looks like other worlds and other dimensions. Words will drop into your mind, not from your conscious self but from the unconscious. A whole new teaching will open up for you. It's so cool, like being back at college; there's a thrill in discovering who you are.

The master—the supernatural master—is within. But it's through the ego, deep into the subconscious mind and then on through that into these cosmic realms of self—that you will find the supernatural energy. It will teach you and show you. Sometimes what it will show you is very practical, such as information about your health, finances, or relationships. Other times it will show general patterns that unfold in daily life. Sometimes it will help bring you an understanding of human evolution and the overall destiny of our people or a heightened perception, an explanation of the position you currently find yourself in.

This is a very heroic time to be on earth. There's a tremendous amount of creativity and change and possibilities. You are part of that. This is a truly wonderful era. Your decision to be here on earth at this marvelous time was one of the coolest spiritual moves you ever made.

Through the discipline of meditation you liberate yourself. It doesn't happen in ten to fifteen minutes. Meditation is a process that you're going to work with for the rest of your life. You may not necessarily do it in the same spot for 24 minutes every day. Sometimes the meditation can be five to ten minutes on the bus going to work, or on a plane going from somewhere to somewhere else. Perhaps, some days you may be too busy to bother with the metronome, but you'll pause and get out of your car and sit on the side of the road somewhere—in a field or under a tree—and just be, in silence.

So, Step 9 of the 33 steps is *Power Comes from Discipline*. Step 10 is *Centering the Mind*. Without these two steps, you haven't got much of a chance, because you'll get inspired for a while, then bit by bit, the ego will win back all of its lost ground and you'll return to where you were before. So, meditation, centering, pondering, and reflecting, working on yourself, and trying to understand is the act of calling upon the power to teach you. It will graciously teach you. It's happy to.

Step 11

Believing You Are
Already the Power

Step 11 is believing that you are already a part of this power—
that you have the energy of the initiate within you and that you
are the power. There's a tremendous difference between hoping
you may become it—hoping you may become a great actor, hoping
you may make a million dollars or hoping you'll marry the person
of your dreams. You've got to belong to the dream as well.

So you have to believe in an infinity that you can't touch, smell,
see, taste, or hear. But, in a strange way, you can gradually learn to
feel it. Because the infinity within you is beyond the subconscious
mind—it is oscillating faster than the personality, faster than the
subconscious mind—it is outside of your normal perception.
Therefore, you're required to become it. That is, understand that
you're it even if you can't see it as yet.

After many years of using the theta metronome for meditation,
I started having fleeting glimpses into other worlds. In the end it
became easy to get there, and I would regularly see the near-death
tube that people who have survived medical emergencies talk
about. In the trance state you simulate death, so once you've
cleared out the crud of the ego, the tube eventually appears. It's a

highway between here and there. Beyond the tube are countless dimensions of evolution. Some are bathed in the God Force; some aren't. When I first saw the celestial light of those worlds, I was overwhelmed. I have never seen so much beauty, so much reconciliation, so much love, all at once. All the inconsistencies of my life were healed in an instant, bathed in the celestial light of God.

But the most startling thing I discovered was that the love that exudes from the light of God is impartial. It is not an emotional love as we understand it on earth, for the God Force has no needs or desires, It just is. It doesn't manipulate or require a response. It's the most beautiful kind of love that exists—unconditional, celestial, and everywhere, because the God Force is everywhere. It's a love that asks nothing in return. It has no emotion or judgment. My reaction to the first sight of that love was extremes of happiness that came from a sense of belonging. Suddenly, finally, things on earth made sense; they had a higher meaning.

The celestial energy at the end of the near-death tube is the same energy that flows through all things—it doesn't really have a comprehension of what you need, of whether or not you have the job you want. It's impartial, like electricity. Electricity can light a church, a kindergarten, a whorehouse, or a torture chamber.

The infinite love of the God Force is a power that seeks no particular end or result, either for Itself or for you. But you can direct It into your life, and you can use It to deliver to you the things you want. You direct It by projecting It outwardly from yourself to others. People respond in an instant. It's no more than pushing acceptance, unemotional love and light. It's you pushing energy so that people can become stronger and more free.

But first you have to internalize it, as I said in Step 4. You have to belong to your goals and dreams. If, say, you want more money but can't internalize that feeling; if you feel lack, if you don't act abundantly; if you are not gracious and generous of spirit; if you're not open and warm-hearted, then the universal law just reflects back to you the cold, tight feeling you emit. You get nothing more than you have now, and things happen to reduce or take away some of what you already have.

It doesn't matter if, from the ego's point of view and in your current economic or social standing, you're not a big person. You've got to start feeling big, regardless—become larger than life. By becoming silently big, you exude confidence, you stand tall for people—not via a pushy attitude, clever dialogue, catchy slogans, and showing off, but in the currency of energy—valuable energy, not verbal diarrhea and wind.

Visualize yourself there in your hometown, standing across it like you're 300 or 500 feet tall, and you're big. The little things of day-to-day life don't bother you. You are beyond them; you don't mind a little rain. You don't mind a few people giving you a hard time in the supermarket. You don't mind the guy in the post office who was rude to you. You don't mind the car that cut you off in traffic. You're not in a rush; you're eternal. You're bigger than these things. You are now standing in an evolution that's bigger than the petty world of the tribal emotion—beyond the personality, beyond the mind.

In the world of the ego, you move along a straight time line—yesterday, today, tomorrow. In the Infinite Self, the future is now. That's why it's so important for you to believe in yourself now, to believe in the power that is with you now. If you are moving toward a goal, see it in your mind's eye, act it out, and feel it granted in your feelings so that it exists in the now. So if you want a new car, you can't suspend it in some ill-defined, distant future place. That's hopelessly difficult for your feelings to grasp. You have to feel that you have it now.

That's why I say, "Hey, if you want a Rolls-Royce, go into the showroom, get inside the car, and start sniffing around." When the car salesman comes up to you and says, "Excuse me, sir/madam, could I help you?" You say, "I've got to sniff my car before I buy it, because I want to know what this leather smells like. I understand that this is some of the finest leather in the world. I want to know how it smells, so excuse me a moment, while I sniff away. As soon as the money materializes, I'll be back with a check, and you can give me that silver metallic one over there."

So you've got to believe, and you've got to feel. When things are distanced from you, you'll never achieve them. The mind says, "Nah! We can't have that." So if abundance is your issue, feel abundant. Somewhere in one of my books I talk about going into a five-star hotel even if you haven't got money. Go into the most lah-dee-dah place in town, and just sit there and have a coffee and drink it slowly. Don't spend a lot of money, but join in the affluence. Be there with the millionaires. Sit in that marble palace, and declare yourself in.

It's by joining circumstances in your feelings that things come to you. By joining serenity, serenity embraces you. Never mind if your life's a mess right now. You can have loads of problems and still be serene, quietly working your way through things. And you've got to feel the Infinite Self even if you're completely victimized by your personality and your ego. You've got to feel abundant when you haven't got any money. It sounds like a contradiction, but it isn't, because the minute you start to feel it, your energy moves up. What we're trying to do here is ratchet up to another place—leaving, waving, saying goodbye, and going to another place in your feelings, understanding and trusting that the Infinite Self is there to guide you. Remember, you don't have to know where you're going in the long term. You just have to know where you're placing your very next step.

Say to yourself as a discipline several times a day, "I'm eternal. I'm universal. I'm infinite. I am what I am." And as you say those words, watch how they resonate throughout your body—throughout your personality, your ego, your mind. And then you'll see the world in infinite terms—when you're not dealing with the finite, when you're not dealing with the limitations, when you're moving out of restriction, away from manipulation, where you're infringing on other people less and less, where you're interfering less and less—allowing people to be. Bit by bit, that infinity comes up within you.

You have to understand that the God Force—this incredible, supreme wonderfulness that flows through all things—doesn't infringe. It doesn't mess with people. It just allows you to be. You can be as silly as you want for as long as you want. God doesn't come up to you and say, "Listen you little twirp, get your act together here." When you're ready, the energy is there.

It's the same with the Infinite Self within you. It's ready. You've just got to embrace it. The way you do so is by letting it become a part of you, and you join and become a part of it. So believing is vital—believing in the miraculous, believing in the righteousness and sacred nature of your journey. Try to see goodness everywhere. Notice the abundance. Notice the beauty. Move constantly to where there is serenity, where the God Force dwells, and away from discord and ugliness. Wave goodbye to restriction, and enter into the tone poem of the warm, gentle wind of the God Force ebbing and flowing through your life. Allow the cosmic nature of the God Force to flow.

Step 11 is believing you already have the power and that you are the power. It requires you to believe in the unbelievable, to observe the unobservable, to become a part of things that humans normally never see. It asks you to step through a door to another world. Come with me now to the next step. I'll show you that place inside of you where that wonderful doorway exists, and I'll give you the keys you need to open it. Let's discuss principles that will assist you in consolidating these ideas in your heart.

The spiritual world is your true place. It's been waiting since the beginning of time, waiting for your return. Come with me. Let's go. It's time. We've waited long enough.

Come.

STEP 12

YOUR WORD AS LAW

Establishing your word as law is important. The mind is used to getting away with a lot of promises it never intends to keep. You tell yourself you'll do this and that, and then you don't. You promise to pay your friend on Saturday, and you forget, or you deliberately duck out of your obligation.

It's important to establish your word as law unto yourself and others, because that in itself becomes an affirmation of your ever-developing authority over the ego. If you say to yourself that you will do something, do it. Don't make promises you won't keep, and don't make promises to others if you can't or won't follow through. Become immaculate. Be honorable. A life without honor is not worth having. Don't commit if you don't have to. If you aren't sure you can follow through, you can always stall others, saying, "I'm not sure; call me in a week." People are used to that.

By making your word law, you develop power. Sounds easy, doesn't it? Most people are not used to their word as law. They are used to wimping out—slip-sliding away if conditions don't suit them. It weakens them, for the mind knows you're full of bull.

As you start to work on yourself, your energy moves faster. In my book *Miracles,* I suggest that the total energy you express as a mind-body-spirit is an oscillation—one that is moving very quickly.

I selected a hypothetical vibration of 20,000 cycles a second as an arbitrary figure to describe the overall oscillation of an average person in the tick-tock rhythm of life.

There's no scientific way as yet to measure or quantify how fast people oscillate, so I picked a figure out of a hat. It serves only as a yardstick. I said, if an ordinary person is at 20,000 cycles per second, a person who's begun to work on him- or herself might oscillate at, say, 25,000 cycles a second; and a person who's very evolved, who has a strong personal light, might be 50,000 cycles. Beyond that, you might guess the energy of the initiate to be 100,000 cycles a second or more. However you quantify it, you are a wave-state that is oscillating through this physical experience.

As you work on yourself, your concentration moves away from the mundane and toward the infinity of spirit within; your total energy moves up faster and faster. Your ability to materialize things in life becomes more and more instantaneous. At 20,000 cycles a second, a person has an idea, they visualize or think about something they want, and $19\frac{1}{2}$ years later it may or may not occur. Once your energy starts going faster, any thoughts and feelings you have become reality extremely quickly.

You think about "the burning bush," and there it is, burning in your hallway—instant karma, positive or negative, depending on your focus. You are now grasping an immense power. Any errant thoughts, and suddenly a large turd is falling on your head from a great height. So your word as law requires you to understand the need to protect your power, and with that comes responsibility—whatever you put out is what you are going to get. So be careful not to use your thoughts and feelings in a flippant way.

Part of this cleaning-up-your-act requires that you don't make promises you won't keep. Don't say to yourself, "I'm going to give up chocolate" if an hour later you'll sit there and munch through an entire box. If you make a discipline—a law for yourself—follow through. If you don't feel confident about following through, don't make the law. When you're good and ready to give up chocolate, you will.

Embrace your word as law, and you'll see an immediate benefit as things begin to pop up effortlessly. But you have to mean what you say, so choose your words carefully—be purposeful, and police what you think and feel. If any crud comes into your mind, pounce on it quickly and change it. Everything is reversible.

Also, don't give people loads of *BS*. Don't talk gibberish. Don't talk about yourself. Come out of your silent power. Listen to others—talk about them. Don't make idle promises, and don't agree to do things you know you're not going to follow through on. Become verbally disciplined; don't show off. Don't boast. Don't exaggerate. Just stay inside what you know is true and real.

Next, get into a truthful dialogue with yourself. In other words, don't buy the *BS* the mind gives you. The mind says, "Yeah, we're doing fine," and you know you're not doing fine. The mind says, "Yeah, we're looking for a job," and you know you're not looking for a job. "Yeah, we're going to handle giving up chocolate," and you know you haven't given up chocolate and you've got no intention of giving it up. When you say to yourself, "My word is law," you establish a dominance, an authority over the mind; so when you say something, you're going to follow through.

Here's an exercise that will strengthen your will and help you along a bit. Pick a spot outside in the garden or in the park, wherever, and find 12 stones. Tell yourself, "I'm going to move these stones ceremoniously every morning at 7:01 A.M. for seven days for fifteen minutes. Then pick up the first stone, walk slowly across the garden, and place it down; bow and say to the stone, "Thank you." Then walk across the garden, pick up the second stone, and take it over to the other side. Place it next to the first stone. Walk back and forth, taking all the stones across the garden. Now, pause for a moment and pick up the first stone once more, walk back across the garden, and put it back where it was originally. Transfer all 12 stones back to that side of the garden again.

If all this seems like a pointless exercise, you are right; it is supposed to be pointless. The mind will ask, "Why are we moving 12 stones across the yard?" You tell it, "Shush, this is a spiritual way of getting stoned!"

You are strengthening your will and developing a personal law. It is irrelevant if the mind likes the idea or not or if the exercise has a point to it or not; the idea is to establish yourself as the lawgiver in the realm of your consciousness. You're saying, "This is my law. At 7:01 A.M. every day for seven days, I will ceremoniously move stones. This exercise has the effect of not only establishing you as the disciplined, dominant force, but it also allows you to override the discomfort the mind may go through.

The mind won't like hauling stones, especially if it's raining. These actions involve work, and they are outside its normal legislation. At this point, you dismiss the discomfort—rather than accommodating the ego—by, say, staying in bed. Set a discipline, like the stones, and do it for seven days. You need to see that your word is the law.

If you don't have a garden near you, you could, instead, move 100 books on and off your bookshelf, dusting each one as you go. Do it exactly at 7:01 A.M., or whatever time you decide; do it for seven days.

In establishing the idea of *My Word As Law*, you improve your ability to materialize things you want in your life. You understand that when you come up with a thought or feeling and when you express it mentally or verbally, it is going to appear in your life. Because you are powerful, you can materialize your consciousness. The boundary between your internal world and the external world has melted—you have less definition. You see yourself as infinite, so the miraculous is not only possible but expected. There is no more inside and outside; there is only one infinite consciousness that describes all reality.

The ego's function is to separate you from others, defining you by creating a mental and emotional distance. As you move toward the Infinite Self, you are exiting the ego's world to join with an inner energy—not just your inner energy but that of all the people on the planet and the cosmic energy in all things. In that joining, you will be able to pull things to you—benefits, opportunities, creative possibilities. You will pull them to you unexpectedly from a great distance.

The ego, living as it does in a limited 3-D world, has to go get things; it has to find things. It is required to struggle to materialize things. It has to force things to happen—it needs to sell itself. Rather than forcing things to happen, see the whole of the planet being inside you, a part of you. When I say to you, "Stand tall, be a big person," I mean, become big-hearted, expand your mind, expand your feelings to incorporate everything. If you are infinite, you are everywhere. Be everywhere. Be everything. Once you are everything—and through the connection of your Infinite Self are connected to everything—materializing things is easy. You are only reaching for different parts of yourself.

So you'll have an idea, and suddenly you're on a train with some person sitting across from you. You think, "My God, he's good-looking. I wanted a soul mate, and here I am sitting right opposite a perfect candidate. Instantly. Perfectomundo!"

When you want to know how fast your energy is oscillating in life, notice the speed at which things materialize. That will tell you if your energy is speeding up or not. As you take to this discipline, be careful what you ask for and what you say. If you say to yourself, "This life is a bunch of crud," plonk, the great goo-goo bird drops one from the sky on your head. If you say, "This situation is a pain in the rear end," you'll soon find yourself buying hemorrhoid suppositories at the chemist.

Since your word is law, never think or talk in terms of things being hard, evil, ugly, or difficult. Avoid words like "impossible," "worrying," "trouble," and "problem." Your problems are not problems; they are challenges. Refer to them correctly and clean up your act, saying, "Hey, I feel great. I'm eternal, I'm immortal, I'm universal, I'm infinite. I feel abundant." When people say, "Do you see the ugliness here?" you reply, "No, I see the hummingbird hovering over the flower; isn't it beautiful?" When people say, "Do you see the depravity over there?" you say, "No, I hear laughter, and I see the chubby legs of children running across the playground."

Police your thought-forms, and don't make promises you can't keep, especially when you're in a dialogue with yourself.

STEP 13

ACCEPTANCE

That leads me nicely into Step 13, which is *Acceptance*. We talked about disengaging from negativity in Step 5. Now I want you to develop a real, individual spiritual evolution by stepping away from resistance, away from the binding conformity of tick-tock and the tribal mind. This is a continuation of the process of disengaging from emotion. Through it you calm your yearning. It's simple; you just have to get it.

Because of the ego, the tribal mind is always uncomfortable. People achieve momentary happiness, but they don't experience the permanent ecstasy of the God Force inside them. They can't feel It. Instead, they consider happiness the act of gratifying the ego. So they indulge themselves, relentlessly feeding themselves with circumstances and things that will keep them happy. What fleeting happiness they achieve by gratification is soon destroyed, for the ego's discomfort comes from insecurity. Giving it things doesn't make it feel secure; it only distracts it. You know that. You buy a new gizmo and you're thrilled with it; a few weeks later it's in the back of a cupboard, and you're on to the next thing. It's a perpetual wheel of discomfort, while the ego grumbles, groans, moans, and constantly yearns for things to be a different way.

Our society is full of people crying out for someone to lift them up—to fix things for them, to provide for them, to keep them happy. People are not interested in generating energy for their own survival and security; they want someone else to guarantee their security. In doing so, they lose their power; responsibility is shifted away from self, where it hurts, to someone else—family, friends, a corporation, the government. The process is called "transference." It's nothing more than the ego screaming to be set free from the agony it's inflicting upon itself. That's why people say the world is ugly. They are perpetually uncomfortable with themselves, perpetually insecure.

To transcend to the graceful beauty of the Infinite Self requires you to take responsibility for yourself. Once you do, you'll see that the pain you suffer comes from your reaction to life's circumstances, not from the circumstances themselves. By changing the way you react, you enter into a spiritual appreciation of life, and a beauty and contentment that is not available in the world of the ego.

Start by seeing this place, this earth, this life, as beautiful, and see yourself as beautiful. Know and trust that all is well with the world. The current state of societies and our humanity is an outcropping of our eternal evolution as spiritual beings. We have only come so far, and the way the evolution is at this time is the way it is supposed to be. It's silly to say it ought to be different. It isn't.

Know and trust that all is well with you. Be satisfied where you find yourself, and be satisfied with yourself. If you're dissatisfied, you're entering the Infinite Self in a perpetually dissatisfied state, eternally frustrated, eternally angry, whatever.

So, acceptance comes as a result of disengaging from the common emotion and understanding that you are not your emotions, and neither are you responsible for other people's emotions. When they express anger, fear, and frustration, that is just the reaction of the frailty of the ego. If you're dissatisfied, it's like having a perpetual itch that you can't scratch. You've got to make these current circumstances right. Roam around your house and say, "This is right." At work, say, "This is right at this moment. Tomorrow it may change." Wander mentally around your life, and make each and every situation right and holy. Tomorrow it may change, but right now it is perfect. The circumstances of your life are an external manifestation of your thoughts and feelings. You learn from them. Bless them for that; don't fight them.

When you stop fighting yourself—when you can accept that the way it is, is the way it is, you're free. Say that to yourself three or four times a day. "The way it is, is the way it is. I accept that." You see, you don't need perfection, just progress. Everything can be gradually changed for the better. Meanwhile, it is the way it is. Once you can come out of acceptance, you're free, completely free, because you're no longer in the emotion, fighting with yourself.

So they'll pay you or they won't pay you. If they pay you, you eat. If they don't pay you, you can go on a fast and lose a little weight. If they show up at eleven o'clock, you'll get a ride to the ball game. If they don't show up at eleven o'clock, you can wait till ten past, or you can cancel going to the ball game, or you can walk. Your husband's having an affair or he isn't having an affair. If he is having an affair, you've got two options. You can bring him home, scrub him down with disinfectant, and tell him not to be so stupid, or you can toss him out and find another one.

The fact is, once you understand that the way it is, is the way it is, you don't have to fight circumstances. You can work on changing things instead, and you don't need to burn energy on resisting. Be humble and, in any given circumstance that causes you to react, buy the solution not the emotion. But first accept the situation. Once you have that clear, there are only two options. They either will or they won't. It's either going to happen or it isn't. If you don't make it to the ball game, you're going to go to the cinema. If you don't do one of those two, you're going to go home to rest and meditate.

There aren't any absolutes, but the mind decides, "It has to be like this. It must be like that. It has to be at 8:15 and ten to nine. It has to be pink and blue, and people have to accept me and act in a certain way." That's just the ego's agenda. You've lent your lawn mower to your neighbor, and you think, "I've lent him my lawn mower. I'm such a good and kind person that I deserve to borrow his motorcycle next Saturday." You develop expectancy.

Then when you ask to borrow his motorcycle and he refuses, you feel offended. Hey, the way it is, is the way it is. Maybe he's not a generous character; he doesn't trust you with his bike. So you shrug and walk away, saying, "I would have liked the motorcycle, but I'll take the bus."

Look at the world and be satisfied. See it as eternal, and understand that you don't have to push against the way it is. If you don't like things, walk away. Generally speaking, it's too much effort to change things. You've probably tried it with your relatives. They are often the toughest to change. You've got to love them as they are. Unconditional love is complete acceptance. If I love you unconditionally, I accept you. If you love me unconditionally, you accept me. That's easy to do when you're being nice to me and I'm being nice to you, but what if I'm treating you badly? What if you're treating me badly? Then you have to become a big person, not be sucked into emotion when people treat you in this fashion. That is the test.

The point to remember is, you can never be free until you disengage. So, allow life to flow as you find it. The way it is, is the way it is. Tell yourself that seven times an hour if need be.

There's a famous story in the Tao about a farmer. The farmer's son broke his leg. The villagers came to the farm and said, "My! That's a great misfortune. Your son has broken his leg; now he can't help you in the fields."

The farmer said, "It is neither a fortune nor a misfortune." A day later, the government troops came to the village looking for young men to conscript into the army. They had to leave the boy behind because his leg was broken.

Then one day the farmer's horse jumped the fence and ran away. The villagers came to him and said, "What a great misfortune that your horse has run away."

The farmer said, "It's neither a fortune nor a misfortune." Two or three days later, the horse came back with a dozen wild horses following behind.

The villagers came to him and said, "It's a great fortune that your horse came back with 12 others."

He replied, "It is neither a fortune nor a misfortune."

Remember the teaching of the Tao: nothing is long or short, hot or cold, good or bad. If you define it thus, you have to ask yourself, "Good in relation to what? Bad in relation to what?" Once you accept and disengage, you're free, and that's important. Part of this acceptance takes us to Step 14, which is to judge nothing and quantify things as little as possible.

STEP 14

JUDGE NOTHING, QUANTIFY NOTHING

When we judge and criticize people personally, we define reality and engage the ego. Light couldn't exist if there were no darkness in which it could shine. Goodness can't exist if there is no evil with which to compare it. So everything is relative. Chapter 2 of the Tao says:

> *It is because every one under Heaven recognizes beauty as beauty, that the idea of ugliness exists. And equally if every one recognized virtue as virtue, this would merely create fresh conceptions of wickedness. For truly Being and Not-being grow out of one another.*

Think about it. If you don't judge and don't criticize, what you're saying is, "I'm infinite. I let people be. I have no knowledge about an individual's evolution. I can't comprehend if what he is doing is good or evil, right or wrong. He certainly may be acting in a way I would not choose to act, but I cannot lay down the law and say it should be like this or like that."

Not infringing on people means not interfering, not offering them information they haven't asked for, not offering them healing they don't need or want or haven't requested, not meddling in their lives. It means allowing people to be as silly as they want for as long as they want—in the same way that the God Force allows you to be as silly as you want. You don't judge.

Okay, there are certain situations where you might be called upon to evaluate, but that is not a personal judgment. Let's say that you are the personnel officer in a corporation and you have to pick one employee over another. That isn't judging one person individually or personally; it's just evaluating the situation—evaluating two applicants for a job and picking which one is more suited. There is a difference, isn't there, between judging, and evaluating and selecting. You're not judging the Thousand Island dressing because you decided to go for the oil and vinegar instead. Selection is not judgment. It's making a choice without an emotion or negative response—which is very different from judging.

When you're dealing with other people, allow them to be. Or, if you don't like what you see, walk away. Or, try to change the situation as best you can without infringing upon them, usually through a good example. Or, talk to them in an affable manner—asking them questions, leading them along gradually to where they see the higher ground through their own perception and volition—and allow them to freely choose that direction.

If you are influential, one word from you could send a person into a totally different direction in this lifetime—it could change their whole evolution. You don't know what they need or what their deep inner spiritual self has decided. They may need high energy, or they may need low energy at this time so they can properly understand high energy at a later date.

Let me clarify the difference between judgment and observation. Judgment is engaging your opinion and your emotion, judging others for an action or for what they say. Observation is nothing more than commenting on what you or others might observe. So you might casually remark in a restaurant that the service is rather slow, as it has taken an hour for the soup to show. You haven't judged anyone personally; you have just observed. That's okay.

Gradually you'll learn not to quantify things too much. That way you get to experience life, rather than define it. If you go and watch a movie and you start to quantify it, discussing it with a friend, perhaps, you put it in a little box, and your perception of it changes.

I was walking along in Philadelphia one day. It was freezing cold, and I was wearing just a pair of jeans and a shirt. There's a meditation I learned years ago where you visualize a little flame in your heart. You allow that flame to expand, breathing in and out, and it warms you; because you're thinking fire, you feel warmer.

So I'm trotting along nice and warm, visualizing the flame. The person with me said, "Aren't you cold?" The minute he said that, the flame went out, and I was freezing. In Philadelphia it can get pretty cold. That day it was minus who-knows-what, with a hefty wind factor to boot. By imposing his reality upon me, saying "Hey, you ought to be cold," I became cold. Right up till then, I was perfectly warm.

So you want to be careful that you don't quantify or impose upon people. Avoid saying, "This meal is very good; this meal is very bad." Just eat the meal. A bad meal should not be an emotional upset; it's a gift. It allows you to realize and appreciate what constitutes a good meal—it helps you make selections. Be grateful.

Do you see how once you don't have to define and quantify

things, you can just concentrate on experiencing them? You're not putting life into a little box. By not defining it, you can go from the ego's world, which is often frustrating, to the pleasing state of just resonating with the Infinite Self. "I am, and I experience life. I don't see it as high and low, cold and warm, dry and wet. It's neutral. Hey, I'm doing rain. I have no reaction. I'm experiencing happiness. I have no reaction. I'm not yabba-dabba-doing and swinging off the chandelier. I'm just content."

I fly a lot. I've now been around the world 97 times, so I've done "airport" in this lifetime. I like to sit and watch people go by as I'm waiting for planes. Try this little exercise. Go to a crowded spot—a shopping mall, an airport, or whatever—and just sit and watch people. But rather than watching them intellectually, watch them from inside the Infinite Self. So, don't say to yourself, "That's a pretty dress, this guy's so tall, she's so short, isn't that child cute?" Don't engage the mind; just observe.

Do it for 15 minutes when you go shopping on Saturday. You'll discover how dramatically it changes your feelings. Suddenly you'll find yourself coming from a place of compassion for people. You'll enter inside their spirituality, inside their Infinite Self. You'll be resonating a feeling of belonging, a feeling of love, a feeling of caring for them. Not caring in the sense that you've got to look after them, but just enjoying the heroic nature of their humanhood rather than putting them into little boxes and saying, "That's an Afro lady, there's a Texan cowboy, etc." They're just eternal spirits—schlepping bodies around like you and me.

It's an interesting discipline because you learn a lot about people by watching. Once you don't judge, a higher sense of awareness comes forward. You begin to touch their inner self, and you observe things about them—subtle information that would not be normally available to you.

During my three-day *Wildefire* seminar, I take the guys out into the local town and I have them touch the subtle energy (the etheric energy) of passersby. I attempt to show the men that the height of their perception comes from their lightness of being. Through etheric knowledge and a few simple techniques, their perception jumps several hundred percent in two hours. By touching, perceiving, and not judging, the men understand more—a door opens into another world. You can do it for yourself—you don't necessarily need me to help you.

Try this: as people walk past, visualize yourself with an extended arm, push the palm of your imaginary hand quickly into their heart, grab a molecule of that person, and pull it mentally back to you. How does it feel? What do you perceive here? Who is this person? Ask yourself, What is the overriding emotion of this individual? Bit by bit, once you have run a hundred or two over time, you become very perceptive; eventually you won't need to mentally reach out and touch people. You'll look and you'll know from the emanations they emit.

So remember: don't judge, don't criticize; know it's okay to evaluate and select, but don't criticize personally, and try not to quantify things. Just experience them.

STEP 15

HOLD ON TO NOTHING

Hold on to Nothing is a tough one. You are an infinite energy inside a body; the things you have around you are not really yours. They are material manifestations of an infinite abundance. So your car, your house, your clothes, are all on rental from the God Force. None of them is yours. When you depart this earth plane, you're going to have to leave them behind.

By placing a lot of emotion into having, you heighten not having, because you limit by definition what you do have. So, everything else in the world falls into the "I don't have that" category.

You come to the earth plane as energy. You've got a body to operate in, and you're generating money to sustain that body, but that is different from generating money for security. There isn't enough money in the world to make the ego completely secure. That's why millionaires pound on relentlessly, often losing what they already have in the chase for more. It's partly a power trip and partly a security trip.

The whole function of money is not to *have* it; its function is to use it. The main reason for generating money is to buy experiences. You want to get to the end of your life with zilch in the bank, and look back and say, "My God, look at this huge pile of experiences," because none of your memories are ever lost. Everything you've ever done is in your eternal memory somewhere. So what you're looking to do is not to covet and acquire things, because that will make you neurotic and often keeps you poor. Come instead from the concept of experiencing. You have to invest in yourself—and you do invest in yourself, because you're investing time and probably money in reading this kind of book, so obviously you do.

Release owning or not owning. If you own some great piece of real estate, well, fair enough. But you don't want the real estate to control you. You don't want the thing to become a burden to you. If you buy a really fancy car, it sounds great. But, in reality, you've got to polish it, insure it, worry about it. How much energy are you putting into the car? It might be better that you have an old clunker you can leave anywhere with a little note on it saying, "Please steal me. I need the insurance money." If you have a Ferrari and you're constantly worrying about who's kicking its headlights in, it controls you.

So when you don't hold on to things, you're free. This also applies to the relationships in your life. "I'm with this person. I'm with her today; that is beautiful. But I don't own her. If she's here, she's here; if she's not here, she's not here. I'm not her jailer." If you give people space, they usually stay forever.

"I'm in this job today, but tomorrow I might be doing something else." When you don't hold on, you're free. The more tight-ass you are about "mine," the more money-grabbing you are and the less you have in the end. What's the point of millions in the bank if you live a miserable life and die the world's greatest tight-ass? The more you defend your stuff through the emotion of "mine," the more lack you'll have, and the more you cut yourself off from the Infinite Self within.

Everything you have is in the care of the God Force. If you

come home and the stereo is missing, you can say, "Ah, they've come for the stereo," rather than getting uptight. It's just gone back to the God Force. Somebody else has it now. That leaves space for another stereo to come into your life. Or it leaves space for no stereo at all. Now you'll have the silence to meditate and think about who you are and what you want in this life. It comes to you and you say, "Yeah, what I really want is a hi-fi store." And off you go. Boom—you materialize a hi-fi store. Then you can say, "Look at all these stereos; I own them all. But I don't actually own them. I'm renting them from the God Force, and I'm going to sell them to other people who also want to rent them from the God Force. What a marvelous system."

So once you understand this concept, everything is transient. By holding nothing, you own everything. Much better. More peaceful. And you can actually enjoy the beautiful car because you're not sitting there worrying about it. You can just smell the leather and drive along and think, Wow, this is cool.

People equate security with owning things. The things you own are, for the most part, like nails you put through your foot to keep you well and truly riveted to the floor. It's stuff. It lumbers you down. Half the stuff you own isn't worth having because it creates a prison for you, not an open pasture for you to run across.

So, start to realize you have nothing. You are nothing. When you can get to the point where you can say, "I am nothing," you're free, because at that point, you're everything. If you define yourself, then there's all sorts of stuff that you're not. Hold on to nothing. Use things, enjoy them, be grateful and give thanks, and when you're finished with them, release them. Then you're free.

As I said, I've traveled an enormous amount in my life. I've got two suitcases and a laptop computer—that's pretty much it. I stay in a country for six weeks, then I leave. I go somewhere else for three months, and I leave again. Then I return to the first country for two weeks, and so on. In the end, my whole life is in two suitcases. I can look at my suitcases and think, "Wow, cool—two suitcases, one for each arm. Three suitcases would be a problem."

I'm not poor. My ex-wives have a large chunk of my money, and my friends have another large chunk, but I've got a bit in the bank somewhere. I use it to create more energy. Strangely for me, I even wound up with a house. It's in Australia. I don't have a residency permit there so I don't go very often. I got to keep the house after one of my marriages—nice lady. I don't live in it, and I don't rent it out. Houses are a bit too stationary for my liking, but I do go there once a year for a few weeks.

It's really interesting, I built the house with loads of trap doors and secret passages; there are over a hundred yards of them in between the walls. The house is mysterious, but not mysterious enough for me to want to stay. I have never been keen on real estate; it weighs too much and it lumbers you down. And the government can always find it. There's nothing sexier than piles of money in the bank that you will use to create energy and buy experiences. You don't have to insure that. In America, the government insures it for you. There's nothing sexier than a woman with her pockets stuffed full of cash—very sexy. Don't hold on to things, because in the end, it's a complete illusion to think you own anything. You don't. You're only borrowing it from God, and one day, God's going to want it back.

Okay. Let's go on to the next step.

STEP 16

DON'T DEFEND

Going on from *Hold on to Nothing*, Step 15, takes us nicely to Step 16, which is *Don't Defend*. You could easily add to that, "Don't explain yourself" and "Don't apologize either." But anyway, let's start with "Don't defend."

The energy of the Infinite Self is the energy of the initiate. Nobody is going to understand it logically, as it exists outside those parameters. Once you begin to get it, intuitively and spiritually, you won't be able to explain it to others, and you certainly won't be able to show it to anybody. The very fact that you do attempt to show it to somebody or you try to explain it, means that it's not it. It's invisible—it's a silent power. It's knowing without speaking. It's acting without requiring confirmation or observers. It's doing without effort. Maybe that is dissatisfying to the ego, but it is the reality of the power. You can't wield it. If you wield it, you become satanic. A satanic energy is limited in its effectiveness, and it turns and bites you in the end; you go down to a grizzly fate.

If you have the power, trying to show the power is an ego trip. The invisible sword falls from you—it slips through your fingers, cutting you as it goes. It's like King Arthur's sword, Excalibur. The sword came from the Lady of the Lake—it came from femininity, silence, the placid lake. Then, because of confrontation and wars and misuse, Excalibur fell from the king's grip and returned to the lake. The infinite power is a silent power.

If you have to defend and explain yourself, you're lost. At the very most, you can say, "I know nothing."

"What are you doing?"

"I'm doing nothing."

"Why are you getting up at four o'clock in the morning?"

"I just like it that way. I'm best in the early mornings." You can't be an exhibition of power, because then your desire for power and for observers comes from an egotistical standpoint. If you're not wielding power, if you're not establishing observers—if you're not falling for the common trap of having to have people observe your spirituality, observe your holiness, observe your goodness—then you can be invisible. You could have an immense knowledge, immense power, an immense goodness, but when you're walking along, people don't know whether you're the greatest initiate that ever lived or just the guy that works at the 7-Eleven convenience store.

You can be inside yourself without promotion, without attempting to elevate yourself, without seeking recognition. And you don't have to defend the power. The power is indefensible. So, don't get into arguments with people, don't bother to discuss it, and don't talk about yourself. Be mysterious, and don't talk about your path. It's like having a bunch of butterflies under your hat. They're beautiful and colorful, and they create energy. If you lift your hat to show people the butterflies, they fly away. So, from here on out, you have to learn to internalize what you know, as well as internalize your life.

Internalizing your life is the process I described earlier where you start to see external life as signs, symbols, messages, and signposts. As you internalize the power, you can't hold on to it. You've always got to let it flow through you, like a golden wind. The power has to flow, and you sure as hell aren't going to get out there and try to develop converts. You don't need to promote; if you have perception, you act dumb. Stay silent, and the power doubles and redoubles.

So don't defend, and then don't explain yourself either. When people say, "What are you doing?" just smile and say nothing. In the defending, in the explaining, you're apologizing. You don't have to apologize for the fact that you decided to take life in a sacred way. You don't have to apologize for the fact that you're silently walking from ego to God.

Okay, if you step on somebody's foot, you can say, "Sorry for stepping on your foot." But what I mean is, don't apologize for your actions, and don't apologize for your beliefs. Don't apologize for the way you are different. Because as you take on these 33 steps, your energy grows very quickly, and you'll soon become distanced from the humdrum of ordinary life. You act differently. Your perception of the world and your life changes. The Infinite Self teaches you things that you can't find in books, and you begin to operate from a silent power and a higher consciousness that is not how ordinary people operate.

Once you are on your sacred path, you don't have to sell anybody, and you don't have to convert them either. By explaining the power, you belittle it. By showing it to others, you're saying you don't believe it—it isn't real; it isn't true; it isn't me. So don't bother with any of that. Just silently internalize it, and know you're growing. When you don't feel you are growing is when you're growing the most. When you engage the ego and you think you're doing fantastically well, you've got your saffron robes and you're clanking your little bell and everybody's watching your antics, that's when you're not growing, because then you're slap-bang in ego-land. Establishing observers and admirers, people to watch you and say, "Isn't she wonderful? Isn't he amazing?" is a need of the ego, but it has no currency in the world of the Infinite Self.

Take the power inside and guard it. Don't defend it, don't apologize for it, and try not to explain yourself to people. Just do what you do. The journey is inner. It is the act of making your life sacred. That takes us automatically to Step 17, which is *Constantly Purify Yourself.*

STEP 17

CONSTANTLY PURIFY YOURSELF

To constantly purify means that you will be assailed on an hourly and daily basis by the ego's perception and its traits, urges, and desires. The mind won't let you take on a new concept, and that's it. It takes you a while to belong to a concept. You can understand a concept like *Your Word Is Law* in three seconds flat. It's easy enough to grasp intellectually, but it's much harder to make it a part of your feelings, a real part of your life.

So, in *Constantly Purify Yourself,* you are looking at being vigilant against the negativity and destructive power of the ego. Be careful with your dialogue, and don't express negative energy when you talk. Be careful and purify your feelings. When you're feeling crazy, pull back and relax. Take a moment to be in nature. Take time alone. Analyze your emotions and get to the root of problems as quickly as possible. It is especially important to avoid anger, as that has the effect of a nuclear bomb going off in your subtle energy. It can really set you back if you don't nip it in the bud quickly.

In my little book *Weight Loss for the Mind,* there's a section that shows you how to process emotions, particularly anger. All anger comes from loss. There isn't any other form of anger. So when you're angry, rather than experiencing that emotion and destroying your energy, say, "Hey, wait a minute, I need to purify myself and guard my energy." Ask yourself, "What have I lost?" You may have lost something tangible, such as your car, or you may have lost something less tangible, such as an opportunity, a job, a friendship. Perhaps you have lost energy or security or status, or maybe you have to give up a mind-numbing rhythm, and the ego is resisting. You look at what you've lost and agree to lose it. If you like, you may set upon a plan to retrieve what you've lost, but generally speaking, when things disappear from your life, it's just evidence that the universal law is liberating you from stuff. Most stuff you lose isn't worth chasing after.

To purify yourself, you'll need to spend time on your own, sifting through your feelings, understanding them. Negative emotion is your ego fighting back. "Hey, what is my motivation here? What do I actually feel?" Get to the bottom of the issue. Then, of course, you're going to have to come up with some kind of physical, emotional, mental, philosophical, and spiritual discipline for your life in order to control the ego—to turn around its negative inner voice blabbing in your ear. I'm going to deal with the discipline side of the 33 steps in a later section of this book.

Purity is staying inside your energy, conserving it and guarding it. You're not going to trash your energy by suddenly eating a whole bunch of junk, by going out for a week or two drinking yourself stupid, or by getting so stoned you can't operate. You're not going to take your energy into places where it will be trashed. You're not going to trash your energy by fighting with people. If a confrontation looks like it's developing, start to walk away. There isn't a fight worth having. The initiate walks away; only the fool stands and fights. Sure you can defend yourself if somebody comes at you physically. But usually the best self-defense weapon is your mouth, 'cause you talk yourself out of most stuff. Your second-best weapon is your feet, as you can walk away even if you've been insulted. A lot of people get hurt unnecessarily when the ego's indignation forces them into a confrontation.

In the spiritual trainings I present in the mountains of New Mexico, we rise at 4:00 A.M. and practice martial arts. We don't do it to attack people and hurt them. We just learn it to resonate a stronger energy and develop confidence, as well as for health and fitness. It's very much like the Shaolin in China, a religious Taoist group that has martial arts as part of their culture. Martial arts helps you feel strong and capable. If you resonate a powerful attitude, you'll never be a victim. Predators pick weak people, not strong, silent types.

Purifying yourself also means you will be constantly vigilant. You're not going to take yourself into places where your energy will be wasted or where there's something degrading going on, where something is happening that isn't a part of the spiritual, noble ideas that you're setting for yourself now. If your friends are ratbags and sleazebags, don't judge them; just love them, observe them, release them, and walk away. The world is full of honorable people who are fun and uplifting to be around.

Always select the highest energy, the strongest place. When walking into a place such as a movie theater, ask yourself, Where is the power spot here? Then take it. By being a policeman of your energy and guarding it, you'll conserve power. So much energy is wasted in dead-ends and futile things, on a lack of concerted action, and worrying, and so on. So, purification is observing what works and what doesn't work. Usually 80 percent of your money comes from 20 percent of your actions. You will have quality actions that bring you money, and you'll have loads of other actions that are just fooling about keeping you happy, or just pretending to be busy, important, or active, but they are not actually getting you anything.

So, purify and watch, and you'll soon see what works and what doesn't. If there are certain people who drive you crazy, try to avoid them. If you think, "Every time I see Harry and Shmarry, I get into an argument with them," think about avoiding Harry and Shmarry from here on out. If you go into a restaurant, for example, and it feels weird, leave. If, as you walk in, the waitress is fighting with the chef, leave. It's a warning. If you're standing in line for the bus and the person behind seems odd to you, move. Let him or her go first, then move to the back of the line.

Purifying your energy is coming from the point of saying: The infinity inside of you is very beautiful and very important, and you're not going to trash your energy by taking it into places where there are copious amounts of sludge. You're not going to trash your energy by doing things that will lower it, such as dysfunctional behavior, food problems, drinking, drug taking. Sure, you can have the odd drink and party down a bit on your birthday or whatever, but just indulge in a little bit of this and that—not copious amounts of sending your energy down the gurgler.

Remember what I said before. The faster your energy goes, the greater your experience in this lifetime and the greater your awareness. But also, there is a greater possibility of your falling from a great height. So, when you have the energy of a slug in a puddle and you're plodding along at 20,000 cycles a second, you're powerless, but you're fairly safe. Once you raise your energy and you're going faster and faster, if you fall out of balance, you're going to fall out of balance extremely quickly. So guard your energy and don't allow things to get out of control. If something looks like it's going to be a problem, fix it quickly. Do something positive that's going to re-establish control.

Some time ago, probably a long time ago, you made the heroic decision to evolve spiritually. The reason you made the decision was because you used up the energy of where you found yourself. It's almost as if, in some sacred dimension, there's a mystical scroll with your name on it saying, "Destined to evolve out of the earth plane." If that is your destiny, why mess around on a side track? Purify, walk slow, and watch your life. And don't allow anything to trash this journey. This brings us to the 18th step, which is *Respect All Living Things; Observe the Beauty in All Things.*

STEP 18

RESPECT ALL LIVING THINGS; OBSERVE THE BEAUTY IN ALL THINGS

A s you develop spirituality within, you'll push against the self-indulgent, rapacious attitude of the ego. You'll be careful not to consume more than you need to. You're not going to trash things just for the sake of trashing them. You're going to have respect for your surroundings, animals, all of nature and, of course, other humans.

It's easy to respect people when you know and love them, when they're your friends. But it's much harder to respect people whom you don't know; it's particularly hard to respect people when their energy is a bit grim. That's the challenge.

The reason why people act in a dysfunctional or criminal way or why they hurt others is because they're victims of their egos. They're victims of a society that teaches us all the strange concepts of importance, glamour, and material wealth. Grab what you can, cheat, rob, pillage, and steal. That's just part of the dis-ease of this evolution. You can have compassion for that rather than a desire for revenge.

If you look at it from a finite point of view, it can really bug you and make you scared. But if you look at it from an infinite point of view, people who are ratbags are just people who are learning to deal with their egos. They may cause a tremendous amount of mayhem in our society, but deep within they are infinite spirits. Somewhere beyond the mayhem of their ego, there is a spark of the God Force within them.

So, *Respect All Living Things* means extending to people at least a neutral respect. You don't have to go out of your way to please people necessarily. You don't even have to commiserate; you can leave them alone. But at least respect people as best you can, and particularly go out of your way to be kind to and respect people when they're treating you badly, or when they are obviously acting in an antisocial way. That means putting away your normal ego-reaction and coming from the love of the Infinite Self.

I can't say that I'm perfect at this. I don't know if anybody could ever become perfect at it constantly. But it's a marvelous thing when you can become magnanimous toward people even if they aren't magnanimous toward you.

The other part of respecting all living things is respecting nature and animals. When I first got on the path, I decided I would like to be a vegetarian because I didn't feel good about eating meat. It wasn't just from the spiritual point of view, but because meat is so pumped full of toxins, hormones, and antibiotics. I thought respecting all living things would include respecting myself, so I became a vegetarian for seven years.

However, vegetarianism is a difficult discipline to sustain indefinitely because there are certain nutrients in meat that are hard to obtain in a completely vegetarian diet. I found that flying around from city to city, hotel to hotel, I couldn't sustain my energy levels while being completely vegetarian. So, after seven years, I eventually included a little bit of meat in my diet, and I still have some meat in my diet. I would say I eat meat once a week, and in very small amounts, but I am definitely no longer a vegetarian.

Nevertheless, respecting all living things also extends to projecting love and care to the animals, not killing them unnecessarily. I don't personally agree with hunting. I can understand if you're a tribesman and you have to hunt to feed your family. But most modern hunters don't really need to go out into the forest and start blowing little animals' brains apart. But that's just my personal opinion, and if you're a hunter, God bless you, and I hope it goes well for you.

But respecting all living things is becoming a big person—extending that love you have to everybody. So when you're feeling a little bit grumpy and you're walking down the street, it takes almost a superhuman effort to be nice to people. However, if you're coming out of that infinity within you, you'll need to be nice to people, as that will be your natural tendency. Be polite, respect others, and don't discriminate against them verbally or even mentally.

Discrimination in any form—racial, sexual, or whatever—definitely isn't logical. Discrimination comes from the arrogance of the ego, which, in fact, masks insecurity and fear. We fear those things that we're not used to. So we tend to think this group over here is more dangerous than that group over there. All discrimination comes from the ego's sense of importance, where it believes its people are more important or better or more creative or more socially acceptable than some other people.

We live on a planet that's an incredible mixture. Yes, there's a lot of evil on this planet; yes, there are a lot of extremely grim people who are quite a ways from making the journey from ego to spirit. But we have an infinite amount of time to evolve. Our planet has at least another four or five billion years before it's used up. You can be assured that if you're infinite, if you're eternal, you'll have patience. If you have patience, you can be magnanimous and know that things will get sorted out in the end and that people will come to a sense of sacredness gradually.

Taking a spiritual view of life gives you an automatic humility. You can't fake humility. You are either a humble person or you aren't. But the wonderful thing is, once you've stopped talking about yourself, showing off, demanding observers, cackling on about your achievements, pushing to the front, and so on, your humility becomes automatic.

The violence of the ego is not just physical; it is also emotional violence. The ego likes to hurt people, to belittle others and put them down. It likes to attack and make people uncomfortable because it is uncomfortable. Part of respecting all living things is controlling the emotional, physical, intellectual violence of the ego.

So don't trash people. Even though you know that what a person is telling you is absolutely ridiculous, and you know they're around the bend and won't be able to pull it off, don't trash them. Try to build them up. Say, "Yes, that's a good idea. You might have to make slight adjustments, but I wish you well. I hope it works."

Try to stay away from the grimness of the ego and the way it tries to destroy others. Respecting all living things is not projecting unnecessary violence against the animals and the planet, and not projecting intellectual or emotional violence on other people. That's the sacred way.

As you enter into that serenity within you—in meditation, prayer, purification, or discipline—you begin to appreciate how enormous the God Force is, how much love is involved, and the authority that the God Force has, just through Its indescribable magnificence. Once you've had even a slight glimpse of that God Force, you are going to be extremely humble.

As I said, I've looked up that near-death tube on a number of occasions. I've seen what that light looks like at the end of the tube—the God Force. There are no human words to describe the magnificence of It. One is lost to explain It. It is utterly the most beautiful thing I've ever seen, and the greatest power that exists. A glimpse of that, and every stuck-up twirp on the planet would sit down and shut up. But even if you haven't had a near-death experience, you will be able to feel the God Force in your heart as you begin to control the ego.

Respecting all living things is understanding this point and the magnificence of it all, while doing your best not to allow the ego to create mayhem for you. Respect the air, the water, the earth, the spirits of nature, the beauty of this planet, and all the unseen dimensions that permeate this physical plane as well. Respect yourself. Through respect we generate consideration and love; we learn about ourselves.

STEP 19

THE POWER RISES FROM WITHIN

The initiate doesn't need to push. This is quite a hard concept to grasp, but let me explain it to you like this. At the regular tick-tock level of energy, the hypothetical 20,000 cycles a second, you have to force things. You have to push, get people to pay attention, make a lot of noise, yearn, shove, promote, and really try hard.

Most of the power you have is internal. As you garner power, you can pull to you all that you need. Rather than pushing to sell things, pushing to tell people about the product, service, or knowledge that you're selling, just allow them to come to you. It's so much easier when you allow life to come to you. In pushing, you tend to move things away from you.

Let me explain it like this. You've had that experience when you've gone into a car lot to try and buy a car. The sleazy car sales-man comes up and is really trying hard to stuff the car on to you, telling you how fantastic it is and how you can't live without it. You'd already made up your mind to buy it, but the very fact that he was leaning into you puts you off; you walk away.

Be careful that you don't have that effect on other people—that you don't push and shove so hard that they deny you just because you're pushing. Once you understand that the energy within you is becoming more rarefied, once you understand that the power is there, you can visualize, and feel the thing you need as part of your life. You can take concerted action.

If you want to heal a situation with a person, you don't necessarily have to tromp across town and talk to him or her. You can fix it on an inner plane. In a meditation, you'd pull the person up in your mind, so mentally he or she is standing in front of you. Say their name, breathe in, hold it for a moment, and exhale, projecting that energy and light toward the individual. Do it 11 times. As you breathe this person in and out, send love and healing to the situation. Next time you see the person, he or she will be different—or will simply be gone from your life.

Years ago, a company I owned was being audited by the IRS. The agent was giving us hell—he'd been working on one tax form for 18 months. Three of us got together at 4:00 A.M., and we visualized the agent real small, in the palm of our hand; we projected love to him, and then we blew a short sharp breath to send him on his way. Five days later, he called to say he was leaving the IRS and could we help him get a job in the local area as an accountant. The tax matter was resolved in a couple of weeks once the new agent took over.

Understand that when you have a problem, the solution is internal, and the healing is internal. You don't have to shove and push to make things happen. The more you don't shove and push, the more you begin to affirm that the power inside of you is valid and real. Not only do you get the benefit of the fact that you stop struggling, but you also benefit from the fact that your serenity, and inner knowing, becomes an affirmation of itself. It becomes a self-perpetuating energy.

Understand that the power is there and you can move it. You can project love, healing, and reasonableness. You can stand tall in silence and just move energy around like a lighthouse. So begin to think in terms of eliminating struggle in your life.

I wrote a book once that was pretty successful, called "*Life Was Never Meant to Be a Struggle.*" You might have seen it in the stores. It talks about going beyond struggle. Of course, all struggle is ego. It is the pain and anguish that the ego creates—yearning and demanding and fighting to sustain itself. Pull back and get yourself into a position that you can control.

If, let's say, your problem is money, start working on yourself. Most people think the way to get out of money problems is to earn more money. How to handle money is to get back in control of the money you do have. So if you only have $500 a month to live on, you have to think of a way to live in circumstances that don't cost $800 a month. There's no point in you making five grand a month if your ego is in control and you're spending seven, because you're still going to be in financial trouble.

If you have a money imbalance, just pull back inside and quiet the ego. Tell it, "Hey, we don't need all these things. We don't need a fancy apartment, we don't need a fancy car. We just need to establish control first." That way we don't have to push and shove to get what we want in life. We can be balanced, take our time, and think about what we're doing; we can develop discipline and move powerfully into situations.

When you have a burning need, it destroys your energy. If you absolutely have to sell things to people, they won't buy it. If you absolutely have to have the job, they won't hire you. If you absolutely have to have particular individuals in your life because you love them, the fact that you're all over them usually makes them throw up their hands and flee.

As you understand that you are the power—the power within—

that understanding grows because you start to act in an inner way on things. Each success gives you more power for the next situation. You know you can pull to you whatever you want. You only have to visualize it, concentrate on it, and know it to be granted.

Come with me now to the next step, and I'll talk to you about a very powerful concept from the Tao called *wu-wei*. Wu-wei is the idea of nonaction. There are a couple of subtle complexities to it, and I think you'll find it rather interesting.

STEP 20

ACTION THROUGH NONACTION

Step 20, *Action Through Nonaction*, rides hand-in-hand with Step 19, *The Power Rises from Within*, but there are certain aspects I can add that are important.

There is a concept in Taoist writings called *wu-wei*. It is the idea that there is a natural flow in nature and in life, and that by aligning to this flow and disengaging the mind, one allows things to rest inside a natural simplicity in order to effortlessly unfold in the space of time. Let me quote you a few more lines from the Tao:

> *Perfect activity leaves no track behind it;*
> *Perfect speech is like a jade-worker whose tool*
> *leaves no mark.*
> *The perfect door has neither bolt nor bar,*
> *yet cannot be opened.*

In Taoist art, as in their thinking, you see their reverence for simplicity; their paintings contain few brushstrokes, simple lines, diffused light, and no heavy clash of colors. You see the idea of wu-wei in their effortless grace and simplicity and in the gentle tranquility that is the hallmark of Taoist art.

Originally, wu-wei, or nonaction, was taken to mean sitting in a monastery meditating for 30 years. It was said that by doing nothing you could gain everything. However, in our modern times, sitting forever doesn't really work. What we can see through this idea of *action through nonaction* is that the initiate is detached—that in itself allows him or her to have power. Nonaction is being outside the emotional molecule of your people—the collective emotion—outside the desires and frustrations of the ego. It's the lightness of touch that comes from confidence, grace, and a settled heart.

For example, as I was saying before, if you want to sell something and you want to push it upon the people, "Buy this, buy that," that is action; it is yang, and forward moving. It presses against others. In contrast, pulling back and subjugating your ego to the needs of others is nonaction. If you're a salesperson or you manage a sales force, you want to tattoo the idea of subjugating the ego on your forehead. Teach your salespeople to subjugate their egos long enough to sell whatever it is they're selling.

A salesperson who goes into a shop and starts talking about himself—if he's all rah! rah! and pushy and all over the customer like a hot rash—people start to get defensive. "What's this guy after?" they ask. They become protective. You need to teach a salesperson to place him- or herself psychologically *underneath* the customer and keep quiet; let the customer talk by asking questions about the person or the business he or she owns. This individual is no longer defensive, and people are always delighted to talk about themselves, especially men. They like to tell you about their triumphs. So let them.

As customers talk, you discover who they are and what they need. In the end, if you can't supply a need, you won't get very far. Who is the customer? Well, she's a buyer, say, at a chain of hardware stores, but first and foremost she's a woman, a mother perhaps, a parachutist, a rock climber, and she collects tapestries. She probably doesn't see her job as a buyer of hardware as the be-all and end-all of her life. In fact, she may place her job quite a long way down the list of things that have real emotional meaning in her life.

Once you've found out who she is and you've related to that and listened and said a few encouraging things, you'll want to discover her needs and wants. What are her considerations? Start with a simple personal question such as: How many times a year do you go parachuting? Soon you'll find out that she is desperate to get away, and she's thrilled because she's managed to book a weekend parachuting in the Rocky Mountains. At this point, the two of you have been chatting for 15 minutes and nobody has even mentioned hardware. You've related to her as a human, and you've held yourself back, subjugating your need to talk about yourself and to sell bolts and screws.

By getting underneath people, you can sell to them more easily because you support them. It's a form of love. When someone gives you their money, they're parting with a small part of their security. Paying out has the effect, at a deeply subliminal level of mind, of causing insecurity. Every cent takes them theoretically closer to financial collapse and an ego-death. If I pay out this money, I will have less. Will I be able to eat? If I don't eat, I'll die, and so on.

People have to be secure in order to transfer their money to you. Never forget that. How you make them secure is to not come at them from above (action, yang) telling them how marvelous the product is and how marvelous you are. Instead, work on their comfort zone first, keeping silent for the most part, leading things along effortlessly by asking questions (nonaction, yin). When you do get to talk, be sure to tell them that everything is cozy, safe, and secure. People need to hear that. Work on their positive energy, and tell them about the good fortune that is about to descend upon them in these exciting and positive times. Then, and only then, mention the dumb screws.

So, nonaction is really the act of watching the ebb and flow of events and getting underneath life. It may sound weird because in the previous session I was talking to you about being bigger than life. Being bigger than life is an inner feeling. Now, intellectually, you're going to put yourself underneath. You're going to humble yourself in the ego's terminology and subjugate yourself to the needs of others, your clients say, before yours—just long enough to make sure they're okay and for you to take the order. By being detached, you see inside people's humanity; you soon understand what people want. Understanding what people want is a way of getting very rich, very quickly.

Here's another example. If your body is sick, rather than being in the emotion—running around in a frenzy, taking tablets, and calling the doctor (action), step back and understand you are eternal and cannot be sick; you are in wu-wei. You are in the nonaction of centering yourself first and thinking through and feeling what is your best move here—what do you really need to readjust to your former balance. Dis-ease is yin; it sometimes comes along to help you see how to balance the yang of life. People mostly get sick from burning their vital power through too much activity, and yang.

When you are balanced, you are always in the right place at the right time; each thing that comes along can be perceived in that light. If you are balanced, you move into a probability pattern that precludes pain and injury. To some, life seems like a game of Russian roulette in which people wander around in a crapshoot.

Some get hurt, some don't; some get killed, others don't; some get sick, and some don't. Of course, everything comes from an externalization of people's feelings. Once your feelings are healed, there is no more Russian roulette.

Once you've accepted responsibility for your life, you can understand the deeper meaning of imbalance, and you will want to go within and examine the deeper reasons why. Rushing around trying to fix the dam after it floods doesn't really work. It involves burning a lot of energy. The source is where you should be; in there you can fix everything. Gradually, your external reality will manifest itself according to your new inner patterns.

So, wu-wei is understanding that you don't have to push. When people rush forward, you step back; when they run, you walk; when they cry out and call for attention, you remain still. If you are not desperate in your needs and wants, no one can move you. You have all the time in the world. Say that to yourself several times a day like a mantra: I am balanced. I have all the time in the world.

The external world you see out there is actually only an extension of your inner dream. It's a hard one to comprehend at first, but once you've got it, it saves you an awful lot of rushing about.

Let's say you're dealing with a friend who's difficult. You want him to change his mind and support a project you're planning. Action would be trying to convince him—standing over him, beating him with logic and expounding the good qualities your project offers. Or, it would be manipulating him with guilt, with remarks implying that if he were a good person, he'd want to be involved. He owes it to you, the village, or society. You helped him last year so he ought to help you now, blah, blah. These arguments are action.

Nonaction is standing inside someone's mind and finding out: what is this person's position, what is he actually saying? Why won't he support me? What does he need? Who is he? Where is he at this point in his life? What is his agenda?

So nonaction is the act of putting yourself and your need to have this person support your project aside, and momentarily stepping inside his mind to discover who he is. Next, you see quite clearly that he, too, is afraid, with too little energy to give of himself, so you don't waste time trying to persuade him. If you need help, it will show up. If it doesn't, you will either manage on your own, or now is not the time to engage your energy in this particular project. Bag it.

Everybody wants something. I know that sounds awful, because we like to think of a world where people don't want things. But the fact is, everybody wants things, lots of things. That is neither good nor bad; it's just the way things are. The ones to watch are those who say, "I don't want anything," because when they say that, it usually means they do want something but their agenda is covert, subtle, and hidden. If they really didn't want anything, they would not need to say so.

Usually what people want is recognition and respect—they want to be built-up and praised; they want to be seen as the good guy, they seek observers and approval. They want you to endorse them and help them feel more secure. Remember, everyone is trotting about out there in the real world avoiding death. That's the main function of the ego. It's not necessarily physical death, but death of a rhythm, an idea, or something they're used to. Give people what they want. If they want you to endorse them, do so. If they need to feel secure, support them. Supply their ego-needs, and they will come to you effortlessly.

Nonaction is a different way of looking at things. It's saying, first I will go within. Rather than building a stockade to protect yourself, go within and feel secure. If you resonate solidity, you won't need the stockade. When people say, "We're building a stockade; the Mongols are coming; why don't you help us?" you say, "I don't need a stockade because the day the Mongols come, I won't be here. I'll be happy to help you with your stockade if you like, but please don't take it personally if I leave a few days before it's finished if that's okay with you."

Why is this attitude possible? Because as the advancing energy of the Mongol army starts to come down upon your village, you'd feel it well in advance. You'd say to yourself, "My subtle feelings seem odd today. I can feel something strange in the vicinity. Last night the sunset looked very red, the birds were strangely silent, and there is more dust in the air than usual. The Mongol army can't be far away. It's time to visit my friend George in Devon and drink tea and chat about horses," and off you go.

So, it's pulling not pushing—a balance of action and nonaction. And, of course, it's the silence of your meditation, the sacredness of your life—that's how you create nonaction. Let's go to Step 21, which is *Dedicating Your Life to the Sacred Way.*

Step 21

Dedicating Your Life
to the Sacred Way

O nce you accept the infinity within you, life becomes sacred. In the world of the ego, nothing in particular is sacred. So, respecting your life and all living things and acting in a sacred way, your actions become an affirmation of your intention—an affirmation of your spirituality and your dedication to the Infinite Self. As such, it's important for you to develop a sacred attitude to life. That will involve religious or sacred rituals that are meaningful to you.

How do you make a thing sacred? You make it sacred by concentrating upon it and basically saying, "This is sacred." Take an ancient religious relic—like you've got Saint Matilda's toenails in a box or something. If everybody in the congregation considers Saint Matilda's toenails to be sacred, they become sacred. Why? Because people agree that these toenails from the 12th century, in this little box, are sacred. That's the only way you can make things sacred. Things become sacred when you concentrate on them, revering them and investing them with a special kind of awe.

So, to make your life sacred, you only have to look at your reflection in the bathroom mirror and say, "This is sacred." Then start acting in a sacred way. Act deliberately; act with intention. If, in any given situation, you can't act powerfully, don't act. Preserve your energy, and don't trash it by acting ineffectively.

Have rituals and ceremonies that you perform. Make them a part of your discipline. The discipline of rising early is a sacred discipline, as is the discipline of prayer, the discipline of silence, and the discipline of looking after yourself. Concentration, remember, is love. When you concentrate on something, you love it. If you want to create a sacred path for yourself, concentrate upon yourself, love yourself, and act in sacred ways. Teach it to others.

A lot of my philosophy has been very much influenced by the Native American tradition. I particularly like the fact that the Native Americans are philosophically close to the Taoists, and, like the Taoists, the Native Americans revere nature. When I go to my spiritual home in Taos, New Mexico, I gather with my friends who are from all different races and walks of life. They're not necessarily Native Americans; some are, but most aren't. But we gather, and we perform ceremonies together. We perform *Talking Stick,* which is a Native American ceremony of prayer and conversation that takes place around a fire. Or we perform *Sweat Lodges* for healing, prayer, and meditation. Sometimes we get together at three o'clock in the morning for a special meditation or some special ritual that we perform at night in the mountains.

We're not a religious order or an ashram; we're just ordinary people. One guy works in a publishing company, one guy's a lecturer—that's me—one guy works at the local garage or whatever. We're just ordinary folk, gathered together, acting out our respect for each other, our planet, and our evolution in a sacred way.

I like to create that sense of sacredness with me wherever I go.

Little things. I don't overdo it. For example, if I'm in a hotel, I'll pull a flag with a sacred symbol on it out of my bag and pin it up in the hotel room. I might light a little candle and place the candle beside the flag. Before I go out to my morning's business, I stop and kneel before the flag and say some sacred things. Maybe I have an intention that day to deliver a product, a lecture, attend a meeting, or go to the bank. So I review it in my mind and see things going well. What I am saying is, "I am in the ego's world, doing ego things, earning a living, and meeting the bank manager, but these mundane acts are sacred to me."

Seeing your life as sacred is no more than developing that attitude and having a place you can call your own. One small room in the house, or even part of a small room, is enough. In that room you place your holy objects—the Bible, the Tao, or something that has been written that you feel has value. You make your chosen spot an altar to the inner self. Then you act that out during the day by seeing the inner self as sacred—seeing this planet as sacred.

Out of sacredness and humility comes a natural sense of gratitude. So take time to be grateful. It's a beautiful and humble thing. It becomes an affirmation that says, "I am in control. I'm eternal. I'm not in a rush. This is a beautiful journey. With all its ups and downs, it's still beautiful."

In aligning to the sacred way, you align to the Infinite Self. Develop sacredness in everything you do. Concentrate on the things you do. Washing the car can become sacred if you make washing the car into a prayer. If you just roll out with some soap and water, it can be a drag. But if you make it sacred—and there's the bucket, and there's the brush, and there's the soap suds, and here's the rags, and they're all lined up, you dedicate yourself to this self-imposed ritual called "washing the car." The act becomes a prayer through which you acknowledge and accept God and your human journey. So, turn your life from mundane and meaningless into sacred and holy, and consecrate it in the sacred way.

Step 22

Understanding That Inspiration and Creativity Come from Within

A s part of this journey on the earth plane, you're going to have to handle survival stuff—cooking food, washing your body, paying the mortgage, and so on. Beyond all that, and beyond your involvement with friends and family, there is one other purpose for you in this lifetime: you have to express and create.

It's a challenge to think up a new idea or write a poem or paint an original painting. Creativity is often uncomfortable, as it requires you to go deep within. However, as you embrace the Infinite Self, you touch not only your inner subconscious self, but, I believe, you tap into the deep collective mind of humanity. There you will find yourself in touch with all the creativity that there has ever been.

I think in neurolinguistic programming (NLP) they call it "modeling," where you think about or notice what successful people do, and you do the same thing. That, in the external sense, would be modeling. I think it's a good idea except that there's a small danger you might wind up as boring and tick-tock as everyone else.

In my lectures, I sometimes ask people to think of an idea that has never been thought of before. There's a long silence. Try it; it's quite hard. But the Infinite Self is ram-jammed full of stuff that no one else has thought of. Also, all the energy of the very greatest creators of the past and present is still all there. It hasn't disappeared.

Creative splendor is infinite. It doesn't waste away. Whereas Mozart is now dead and buried, the inspiration that was Mozart is still alive. So if you play or compose classical music, you can pull upon the memory of Mozart—his energy—and you can use that as an inspiration to improve your music and to make it more original. All of Mozart's energy is still in the collective unconscious—in the perpetual global memory of our people. You can call upon it and tap into it. If you need his energy, study his life, listen to his best works, and then, from the familiarity of understanding his genius, enter a meditative state and just ask to be locked into his inspiration. Say, "Amadeus, bro', show me a few cool riffs on this guitar that no one has ever heard before." Play what you hear in your mind.

Once you understand that creativity is infinite, you can see the benefit of putting the ego to one side and allowing subtle ideas and feelings to flow from within. There is a huge difference between intellectual thinking and inspiration. Modern paintings are a good example; they are often urban, negative, and intellectual, which makes them busy and neurotic. They don't necessarily please you—often they repulse. Then you see a simple painting of a child sitting in the dirt by a railway track, and it's very beautiful because you can see the simplicity and the pathos; you can see the emotion, and you relate to the feeling. Stay away from the mind; it will bore everyone silly. Reach for the God Force; reach for the impossible, and have the courage to express yourself in a totally different way.

Creating is not necessarily painting, music, art, or books. It can be carpentry, bricks, nurturing children, education, sport, and healing. But, however you choose to express, you are here to create. The way to start is to discipline the ego. You need order and silence, and you have to be in touch with your subtle feelings; then instant prolific creativity comes up from within.

Most of what people create is fairly boring, isn't it? So they think it through and say, "Well, this guy painted the tree green and to the left, so I'll paint it greeny-brown and put it on the right." People look at it and think, "There's a greeny-brown tree on the right—yawn, yawn."

Real creativity is an inner thing. Once you go past your resistance to creativity, past the natural laziness the mind has—you get settled and ready to create, and it's amazing how prolific and original you can become. The ego-mind will slow you down; it will make excuses. It will worry about how others might react. Worst of all, it is lazy and disorganized. But your feelings, your infinity, isn't worried or lazy—it flows endlessly; it's original. So put your thinking aside and call upon your subtle feelings to show you a new originality and fresh ideas, or even an old idea that you can express in a new and different way.

If you want to create, get the tools around you that you need. Lay out your paintbrushes in order, in a sacred way. Bless your paintbrushes. Give thanks for your paintbrushes. Give thanks for the colors. Put your paintbrushes in a special place. If you say, "I'm going to paint at eight o'clock because my word is law," then go and sit there, settle, center within, and feel the painting complete and finished. Up from your feelings will come a painting that is unusual, strange, different, and complete. All you have to do is rub the brush on the canvas a few times. People will love to buy your work, or it will just give them pleasure.

Rollo May wrote a great book called *The Courage to Create,* in which he said that we have to go beyond our natural inhibition. The ego has enormous inhibitions about creativity because the ego hates to be evaluated. It wants to paint something neurotic and complicated and have everyone adore it and praise it. The ego is very keen on things like "its expression" and "its art"—"This is my statement. I'm not going to change for anybody else; I'm going to do my slightly green tree over on the right. This is me. I am terribly important and neurotic and everybody should stand up and salute."

There are loads of writers, artists, painters, and creators who are full of bull. When you listen to that dreary stuff about "my art" and "my poetry" and "my film," it always makes me want to throw up because it's so ridiculous. The fact is, if you get within yourself, you don't want to be inhibited. You just want to create. People are going to like it or they're not going to like it. But if you have to sell your creativity, then you might have to adjust. There are loads of artists who are suffering from an eating disorder called *too much ego, too little God Force*. Sometimes you have to adjust if you want to eat.

I've found I've had to do that over the years because if I really wrote the books I wanted to write—the ones that were deep inside me—people wouldn't understand them. So I've had to write books in a language people can understand. That's just a matter of merchandising. One day when I've got a minute, I'll write some books that tell the story of the inner worlds. If people don't understand them, it won't matter because they'll have all the other books to read in the meantime. That's just one of the compromises I've decided to make.

Anyway, creativity is one of the main reasons for being on the earth plane. Think in terms of "What will I create?" and then feel it out. Sooner or later it's very likely that you're going to have something brand new to sell. You've painted something, you've carved something, you've written a program on a computer, you've created some music. Creativity is money in the bank. You can become prolifically creative once you get the ego out of the way. So get organized, be creative, silence the mind, and feel out what direction suits you.

Be courageous. It doesn't matter if you have to do ten, fifteen, or twenty absolutely grim paintings and trash the lot in order to create one that is beautiful and that you can keep or sell. Creativity is a discipline and a way of expressing beauty and the God Force within. Seek, observe, and then try it out, but do something. You'll be amazed by what you can do.

STEP 23

ALWAYS MAINTAIN FRESHNESS; WATCH NATURE, ALIGN TO NATURE

As you exist—in your neighborhood, in your job, in your home, and with your friends—you have to constantly pump energy to sustain the situation. When you feel bored and fed up and stuck, what it means is that you have used up the energy of the place where you find yourself.

You know how when you first go to a new neighborhood it's really exciting? There is a really cool cafe on the corner, neat people, there's a Jamaican band playing at the bar on Saturday night, and you're really pumped up. After a while it all starts to lose that energy. You go into the bar where the band's playing and there's a cockroach walking across the wall, and the little cafe isn't so cool and the people aren't so neat anymore.

This is because, if you are alive and fresh, you use up energy. If you're just tick-tocking along at the slug-in-a-puddle speed, you can stay in a place forever; it really doesn't make any difference. But if your energy is alive, you're going to use up people and places and philosophies, different diets, disciplines; you're going to change cars, change your clothes. Keep staying fresh, and when you see the energy around you dying, move, change, or enliven it. Paint it a different color, move into a different neighborhood, act differently.

Watch nature, because it's your great teacher. It moves and flows and moves on again. There is this incredible beauty out there in the mountains, in the forests, to teach you its silence, its beauty, its humility. Stay aligned to that.

Adjust to the rhythm of the seasons, understanding that winter is not the time to be starting a new project. In winter, you turn inwards, think, mend things, and get ready. Now that spring is here, you can pull energy from the sun, the flowers, the rushing streams, and the buds that sprout. Realize that now is the best time to start the project. Move and put your energy into the spring. Now comes the summer; it is harvest time. You will collect the money that is due to you, sign the contracts, and complete the projects you began in the spring. When you see the leaves turn golden brown and the autumn or the fall is upon you, take time to think in terms of, "Hey, what kind of crud did I collect this year? What needs to fall away?" As you watch the leaves fall, feel the process inside your heart. "Yeah, I can release things, I don't need to hold on; this stuff is finished with, this stuff is stagnant, this relationship is over." The things you've finished with, pass them on to someone else. Some of the things may be valuable, and you may want to sell them. If not, just give them away. They're on rental from the God Force, and you give them to somebody else. Say, "Here, I've finished with this coat. You have it, Harry."

By watching nature and aligning with it, you align to that infinity within you. Nature has no concept of death—that's why the world of animals is pristine and beautiful. An animal can experience momentary fear as it gets itself into a situation where it is vulnerable, but the cow in the field isn't sitting there thinking about its life insurance policy. The cow is just being. It is. It's alive, munching grass, walking around, standing under a shady tree. That's the eternity of the cow. That is the eternity of the raven. That's the eternity of the little crawly things in the earth. They are free of ego, so they don't have a concept of dying. Therefore, they are free of agony.

From nature we learn serenity, and we learn security. We learn a stability that comes from moving and flowing. As you stay aligned to nature as much as possible, you learn from it. You may want to try the discipline that I tried, which was rising at four every morning for three years and walking in silence in the forest while it was still dark. You don't have to do it for three years if you don't fancy it. You can do it for a week. But by noticing, and staying with the natural rhythms of the planet—the sunset, or the sunrise if you're up before dawn—you're ready. You're in a quiet energy. The rest of the world isn't up, their ego and their mind haven't polluted the psychic atmosphere around you. Then you're ready for the day. "I'm eternal, I'm immortal. Here comes the sun. I'm ready."

As you watch that and learn from it, you constantly police what is fresh, what needs changing, what needs energy. If a friendship is starting to fall apart, it's probably because you haven't put any energy into it. So call that person, invite him or her out, and meet for coffee. Put energy into the places where things are getting sluggish. Anything you've finished with, release it and let it go.

There's a little rule that a teacher friend of mine, Denise Linn, lives by. Her rule is that anything you haven't used or handled— that is, touched—in the last six months and that you're not going to use in the next few months, get rid of it. Give it away. What that says is that you will only surround yourself with things that are alive with energy—things you touch, love, and maintain—things that you are using. Everything else: you're going to liberate yourself from the weight of it.

In this way, you remain simple. Look at the birds. They don't have garages full of stuff. They're simple and they know. They wake up in the morning, and they're not thinking, "How am I going to make it today?" They just fly around and peck here, peck there, and the God Force provides for them. Understand that there's an enormous abundance, so keep your life uncluttered, uncomplicated. Keep it simple and ordered, and constantly move toward the simplicity of the Tao.

Come with me to the next step, and I'll show you some concepts that will liberate you from 90 percent of the anguish in the world.

STEP 24

FEAR NOT DEATH; ACCEPT IT, LIVE LIFE

From the ego's opinions come its considerations and needs. From its considerations and needs, come all the contradictions of life. Because it has considerations and needs, the ego can be contradicted. Contradictions create anguish and emotional upset.

By being less rigid, having fewer absolutes and opinions, and working on your emotions and desires, you can eliminate 90 percent of the anguish in your life. Of course, the central anguish we have to eliminate is the fear of death.

Most people have one or two death thoughts every hour of their waking life. It's not actually physical death—the act of leaving the earth plane physically—but, as I said before, it's the death of *things* that scares them—death of relationships, death of a rhythm, change of every sort.

As you begin to embrace the infinity within you, you can avoid most of the anguish of life by being free inside yourself—even if current circumstances don't allow you to be completely free as yet—by accepting flow and by accepting that today you're here, and tomorrow you're not necessarily here. One of the meditations I would like you to do as part of expanding your awareness is to imagine yourself floating up through the atmosphere, into the stratosphere and beyond, and turn and look back at the earth. Now, in your mind's eye, move the earth forward to some future date. Look at the planet below you, and take a moment to see how the planet would be in, say, 200 years' time. Observe the planet with you not there.

It's a powerful exercise. As you observe the planet continuing and evolving, children are born, events are happening, societies are rising and falling, love, mayhem—it's all going on, and you are not present. As you observe the world with you not present, you can see the state of our evolution when you aren't here. You can come to an acceptance of the fact that being here and not being here in the infinite sense aren't any different.

You have contributed to the world mind. You've contributed to the emotion. Hopefully you'll contribute in a positive way to the spirituality of all our people. You are a memory, an eternal memory, so you will be eternally remembered, not necessarily by people who are alive 200 years from now, but in the Akashic Record, in the totality of our human evolution. Your place is there. It's sacred, holy, spiritual. It's a part of all things.

By meditating from above, you get to the point where you realize: one day I will not be here, and that is okay. By not being fearful of death, you make death a friend. In your meditation, you can go down deep inside yourself and visualize your negative attitude toward death as a grim little gremlin that's rather bothersome, constantly running around causing trouble. Make death a friend, dominate it, and get it to walk with you in this life. That way you can put it to one side and accept it without any resistance.

In your mind's eye, call the gremlin of death over and tell it you want to kiss it. Run your fingers through the gremlin's hair and pull its head back and then kiss it—and when you do, bite its tongue out. Spit it out and push the gremlin down, make it sit in a corner. Say, "Listen, you little tongueless brat, you sit here in silence till I call for you, and don't bug me. When I'm ready, we'll go to the next dimension hand in hand, as friends and heroes. Please don't take it personally, me biting your tongue out, that is—I love you. Wait here. I'll be back for you one day.

Half of the fear of change is the fear of not knowing. By now you will already be in a state of not having to know. You don't have to know all the time. So if you don't know how it feels after death, it doesn't matter. You didn't know what life was going to feel like till you got started. So accept, and pull out of the insecurity. It's a part of the ego's legislation to kid you into thinking that death is grim and life is much more desirable. But no one knows that to be true. In fact, the glimpses I have had of the celestial dimensions are so utterly beautiful and beyond human imagination, so full of love and serenity and goodness, that I'd put my money on death being rather more fun than life.

As you pull out of the insecurity about death, it makes you more comfortable with change of all sorts. Nothing is permanent. Enjoy your relationships while you can. They may last a lifetime; they may not. Enjoy the place you are in while you can. It may last a lifetime; it may not. Enjoy the job you're in, and know that when things change, they change to help you. They change to liberate you, taking you to a different place, a higher level of energy.

Don't hold on, and don't worry about things coming and going. If you try to hold on to people, you suffocate them and they flee. Remember, love is like the number 49 bus that runs down through London, along Kings Road, down Oakley Street, and over into Battersea. There will always be another one along in a minute.

There are two-and-a-half billion people out there of the opposite sex. If you're bisexual, there are five billion to bat at!

So, there isn't any shortage of love. You can find another partner. The person you are with isn't absolutely, totally the only one there is, especially if your energy is going up. If you're a slug in a puddle, then it might be tough for you. People are attracted to energy, because energy is life. Energy is the only real security. When you create energy, you create life for yourself; and if you create energy for people, it heightens their security. It makes them feel safer; they respond positively. People are petrified of death, and the ego takes to the job of keeping one alive with an enormous amount of emotion and anguish.

So, what will you do today to affirm life and create energy? Is there a friend you can ring up, inspire them a little, or cheer them up? Is there something you can paint today? Something to clean? To freshen up? What can you do for your physical body? What can you do for your emotions? What can you do today that says, "I embrace life"?

Get used to this idea of the planet in a condition with you not being here. Bit by bit, the fear begins to back off. Say to yourself, "I accept being here; I accept not being here. There is no difference in the condition, because there is no high and there's no low. There's no life and there's no death, just this perpetual infinity inside me."

As you retreat from the ego, leaving most of the intellect and logic behind, you will not care anymore. It's only the intellect that seeks to live perpetually. It's only the intellect that has fear. In the Infinite Self, you can't die. You will never be more alive than the moment after you're dead. It will be an amazement to you.

One of the other things you're going to find out is how light you are—because the physical body is jolly heavy to schlep around. Every morning you wake up and you think, "Oh, God, I've got to schlep these 180 pounds everywhere today." Gravity is grave. It pulls you down to the earth and makes you exert muscular effort. If you've ever had an out-of-body experience, the first thing you notice is the incredible lightness of being. So develop that lightness of being. Be a spirit, rather than a dumpy, heavy, physical ego. Take life in a light-hearted way—laugh a lot. Be responsible, be ordered, be disciplined, but laugh, laugh, laugh. Remember, seriousness is a disease of the ego.

When you meet people who are terribly serious, they are either arrogant or insecure or both. Often they are trapped by their intellect. What happens is, over a period of time they begin to buy their own intellectual cleverness. In the beginning, that works very well, and you get to see how marvelous they are. They can impress people with their knowledge and intellectual brilliance. But then gradually there is no place for the mind to go. Its influence peters out.

Einstein invented everything he was ever going to invent by the age of 25. The rest of his life was spent in a futile chase to find a force he couldn't find called the Fifth Force—the unifying force. He died a bitter man. He couldn't get to God through his mind. What happens to people who become terribly cerebral, intellectual, and serious is that they make their mind their god. And bit by bit the mind can't sustain being God, because there's a limit to what the intellect can discover and know. In the end they become angry and fearful.

So if you really fear death, you've probably made your intellect your god. Take the mind to one side and tell it, "Hey, intellect, you're jolly handy when it comes to working out bank balances, but you're not God. You're just a mind, and there's a limit to how much you are going to discover in this lifetime, and there's a limit to your usefulness. So back off and shut up."

Coming out of the intellect only, and ignoring Spirit, you destine yourself to eventual stagnation. It can make you bitter, angry, and frustrated when others don't acknowledge your mental manifestations as highly as you do. There will be a tendency for you to swoop down on others from a great intellectual height, and they won't react well to that. They will resist as a self-defense mechanism.

The journey is one of traveling from the neurotic aspects of the intellect to becoming a real person who is living in the truth. Accept what is real and true, and you begin to bury the ego—with its enormous arrogance—which tries to make itself into a false god. "Thou shalt not have false gods," and the false god thou shalt not have is your intellect. Return to spirit, and the infinity within you is there—beyond coming and going, beyond life and death.

STEP 25

AVOID BECOMING A GURU

As your energy starts to climb and you begin to release the crud from your life and move toward the Infinite Self, you are going to become a teacher. You may not stand on a podium and teach, or write books, but you will teach, nonetheless. You will teach by example, by energy. You'll teach others because you know the Tao, and you know patience and know the art of doing and not doing. When you become a teacher, I want you to be careful that you teach out of humility, as a magnanimous person.

I've been in the sphere of the human-potential movement for many years, and I've met probably 75 to 80 percent of all the most famous gurus, writers, motivationalists, and psychologists that are currently in the thick of things. If they're on the seminar circuit, or they're well known for their books, at some point I would have probably met them. Some of them are incredibly beautiful people. They are human, they have their weaknesses, they fall as humans and rise again, they're real. But a small minority in the field are utterly grim, pompous, manipulative, hypocritical, and under normal circumstances it takes all of your detachment and resilience not to throw up—I'm talking up-chuck city here. Why?

They raise their energy, people are drawn to them, then they use that power base to sustain themselves. They become money-grabbers and are full of themselves. Or, they think their philosophy is the only philosophy that exists. There is no one philosophy. Philosophy is common to everybody; it's part of our greater knowledge. You can't say, "This is my philosophy," particularly, or this philosophy is better than that philosophy. Some are preferable—in the sense that they liberate. Those philosophies are more useful to you and me than the ones that restrict. But all of them serve a purpose. Restriction serves a tremendous purpose because it allows us to comprehend freedom. Manipulation serves a purpose because it allows us to eventually become magnanimous. You can't have one without the other.

Traveling around and meeting the teachers, you can see how some of them literally buy the idea of themselves being God. So they stand there and attempt to do God for people. They don't do a silent *I am God* like in Step 1, where they internalize the idea and are humble. They stand on stage doing serious amounts of "Look at me," couching it all with a fake humility and cheesy grins and phony displays of purity and love, while deep down they oscillate extremes of yuk.

As you become a teacher, be careful with your energy. You don't want to raise your energy, then come to the end of your life and look back and see how you manipulated weaker people. Using your knowledge to frighten people, to scare them into giving you their power or their money, is not appropriate. Avoid becoming a guru. That's what this all comes down to, because if you are a saintly person and you are a powerful person, the last thing you need is a bunch of people kissing your feet. You've got to be terribly imbalanced and seriously out to lunch to go for that.

I appreciate that in the Hindu philosophy, they revere gurus. I respect the Hindu ways. But for a Western person, forget it. That isn't our game, sitting in an ashram kissing some character on the foot. Teach from energy. The greatest teaching you can ever offer is your example. It's you as you. Strong and solid. When people say, "It's awful, it's terrible, everything is falling apart," you say, "No, it's not; it's rather beautiful. From this falling apart there will come a change, and from that there will develop more."

Stand and teach from energy, by example; serve humanity from inside your silent charisma, your silent power, your knowledge. Teach people and build them up, and then be sure to let them go. Remember, you can't pick them up, because if you do, their little legs will dangle in the air. Instead, get underneath them and support them, push them up, and figure out who they are and what they need.

Teach from truth, teach from energy, teach from humility. Don't be seduced by power over people, by money, showbiz and glamour, because one day you'll drop dead and you will be seriously embarrassed, standing in the light of God, watching how you had the indescribable audacity to set yourself up on earth as a god. Don't use your power over people sexually or psychologically. Don't use fear. Don't rip people off. People on the path are often vulnerable and trusting. Respect that. If you falter on these rules, forgive yourself and promise to be more correct in the future.

Take each person that is pulled to you to the next crossroads, kiss them on both cheeks, and send them on their way, wishing them Godspeed. That is the sacred way.

STEP 26

PHYSICAL DISCIPLINE

I'm sure you understand now that the journey toward the Infinite Self is one of discipline. It isn't an easy journey. On TV, people promise you the world. Send $39.95 and you can have thin thighs in 30 days. You can have this, you can have that; they tell you it's effortless.

The spiritual journey is not effortless; it is a tough journey because it's the journey wherein you're going to wrestle the ego into control. It involves discipline. How much discipline you can impose upon yourself is up to you. At the beginning you need enormous amounts because the mind is tough. Later on, you can forgo quite a lot of the disciplines, because by then you will have gotten into absolute control of your mind and your emotions. You will have a very strong sense of that infinity within you, so the disciplines can be eased off.

But without discipline, you really don't have much of a chance. So you have to agree to the disciplines—or at least some of them. Steps 26 to 30 are the main disciplines you need.

This step, *Physical Discipline,* is understanding that this physical body of yours is a manifestation of that infinity within you. As your energy moves up, you're going to have to become your own healer. You need to understand the physical body—learn about it and care for it. You're going to have physical disciplines not only to heal your body, but to refresh it—and to expand its capacity to absorb the new power you are creating so you can take it to a new place. You have to make it ready to accept the power. Otherwise, the God Force can burn you if you're not ready. And you need the physical discipline to calm the emotions and control the ego.

The first of the physical disciplines is to understand, study, and know the physical body. I've asked people in my seminars to put their finger on their pancreas. About 50 percent of people in the room don't know where their pancreas is. One woman put her finger behind her ear. If you think your pancreas is behind your ear, forget it. You haven't as yet come to an understanding of this evolution. So if you don't know, get a book on the organs of the body and study a little bit about how this thing actually works.

Then you have to take the body into some kind of nutritional discipline. One of the easiest ways of controlling the ego is not giving it the things it craves. Discipline means moving from a diet that is ego-related, unhealthy, and dysfunctional, to a more rarefied diet where you're eating less and sustaining a more alkaline diet. Carbohydrates, fats, oils, and proteins are very acidic. You don't need a lot of acidity in your body. In fact, the perfect diet is more than likely going to be 80 percent alkaline foods and 20 percent acid foods. If your work is very physical, then it will be 30 percent acid and 70 percent alkaline. The alkaline foods are all the foods that don't satisfy the ego. Fruits and vegetables are naturally alkaline.

What you have to do is begin to reduce the acidity in your body in order to have a balance. As the energy goes up, you'll become your own healer. You won't be able to schlep your body around to the local doctor, because the doctor is going to come out of pure tick-tock. There's nothing wrong with modern medicine, but in the end, you're your own healer. The point of physical discipline is that if you can maintain it, if you can begin to create a physical discipline, your energy rises very quickly. There is no one particular thing you can do that is more powerful than physical discipline.

That involves exercise. It involves understanding your physical body and getting control of it. You don't want to be too harsh on yourself, though. People who have very rarefied diets actually wind up getting very sick. What happens is, their body becomes so pure that it reacts to everything. They become allergic to fumes, paint, toxins, dyes, and various ingredients that are in foods. They become allergic to the whole of life. I know people who have gone on extremes of nutritional disciplines. They've started off having a tremendous amount of energy, because the body detoxifies and becomes purer, but bit by bit they come into the law of diminishing returns. Their body becomes so pure that it really doesn't have any crud to work on. It begins to react to everything outside of itself, and the people become hopeless. So the cure for that is to start eating a bit of crud if you're so refined that you're ill and allergic to everything.

Going on from the physical discipline, and studying the physical body, understand that you can direct energy and light into your physical body during meditation to enliven and heal it. As its energy is going up, the cells will oscillate with more power, so give it as much rest and balance and alkaline food as you can. Don't strain it.

The other thing that is marvelous for controlling the ego is fasting. When I first started on my spiritual path, I fasted for two days every nine days. Then twice a year I fasted for five days. I still fast from time to time. What's beautiful about fasting is that it really quiets the mind. Eating is how the ego feels secure that it isn't dying. When you fast, the ego gets very quiet.

There are loads of good fasts you can choose from. You don't necessarily have to fast with a total absence of nutrition—you can have a fruit-juice fast, and you should drink lots of water. In fact, most fasts are better if you drink loads of water, as it helps you detoxify. Or, you can drink vegetable juice. I take a load of vegetables, especially ones that are high in potassium, and make up a soup of potatoes, green beans, onions, and so on. I boil it up and skim off just the juice and drink that during my fast. Fasting really helps you take control.

Of course, it works as a weight-loss technique, but although you might lose a pound a day while fasting, it's really easy to put the weight back on again when you start eating. However, it certainly allows the whole of the digestive system to relax and release.

If your digestive system is slightly out of control, fasting is a great way to bring it back. So try it. If you've never fasted before, just try a one-day fast, and say in a sacred way, "I'm going to fast on Saturday." It's good to pick a weekend or a time when you're not working, because then you're on your own, and you can take time out in nature. You could do a one-day fast, leave it a week or two, then do a two-day fast. Once or twice a year, do a five-day fast. If you have blood-pressure problems, or blood-sugar problems, you should get the advice of a professional before you begin your fast so he or she can advise you on the best way to handle it.

Once you stop eating, the body begins to eat itself. What it eats first is the crud. If your body feels imbalanced, one of the simplest ways to heal it is to fast. So while the body is eating the crud, the mind is also quiet. So you can really get in touch with what your body needs. You'll know which vitamins and minerals you're missing and where the toxicity is—you'll be able to seek out the treatment you need.

Obviously, don't use fasting instead of proper medical advice if you have a serious medical problem. Use the technology that's available if you need to use it. But most everything that goes on in your body in a day-to-day sense is fixable.

Once you've handled physical discipline, come with me to the next steps, and I'll talk about emotional, mental, and philosophical disciplines. These will help with how you handle fear and process feelings so you can liberate yourself from debilitating opinions and step into a more infinite perception.

STEP 27

EMOTIONAL DISCIPLINE

I've talked a lot about emotion in this 33 steps concept, so I don't have to go into it a great deal. But there are a few things I'd like to discuss in relation to emotional discipline.

The tribal emotion is common to tick-tock and the tribal evolution; you have to understand that and be compassionate. People are going to be out of control. The fears of the ego will dominate their every breath; you have to let them be without judging or criticizing them. The discipline is to begin to distance yourself from the common emotion and develop an emotional reality of your own. So when you see newspaper headlines such as, "Inflation Shock! Economy Worsens," you don't get sucked in. In fact, if you buy the stupid paper and read it, you find inflation has gone from 3.11 percent to 3.15 percent. It's no shock at all and isn't going to make a blind bit of difference to you.

The trick is to stay balanced in a society where the government and its financial policy is bouncing around perpetually. None of that stuff's getting any better, is it? So don't get sucked into the emotion of lack. And don't get sucked into your own emotions. Remember this: when you feel negative emotion, immediately nip it in the bud.

Extremes of negative emotion are like a nuclear bomb going off inside your metaphysical energy. You have to control the balance fast. So as soon as you find yourself getting out of control, pull back and sit down; visualize yourself standing above yourself, look back at this lovely person that is you, and ask yourself, "What's upsetting her?" or "What's he angry about?"

All emotion comes from the ego's resistance to the contradictions of life. Most suffer from confusion. They are never quite sure if they have chosen the right path or not. Shall I? Shan't I? Will I? Won't I? All confusion comes from asking questions. You have to ask a question in order to be confused. Think about it. Confusion comes from complexity. If your life is very complex and you're asking yourself loads of questions, you'll be confused. If you want to heal confusion, simplify your life, take a minimalist approach, and ask fewer questions. Just be and flow.

Anger comes from loss. You've got to lose something to be angry. So as soon as you feel angry, sit down and figure out what you've lost, and agree to lose it. Frustration comes from the intellectual disease of having to put things into time frames and conditions, trying to fit your life into comfy little boxes that aren't necessarily reasonable. So, frustration is a disease of not understanding your Infinite Self, not understanding change, limitations, and time.

If you don't have enough time to do all the things you need to do, it's a sign of your lack of control. It's a manifestation of a lack of good boundaries. You have to set boundaries and get rid of some of the things you've chosen to do, or reduce your obligations. You have to pull back and get control by eliminating the less important stuff and staying with the actions that are comfortable and reasonable. Being a workaholic is a disease of the ego. It often comes from a poor self-image, which requires you to overachieve to win approval. Don't become a power freak, and don't become a money freak. Get a life first, and do the other stuff as much as you need or want to—everything in moderation.

Back to emotion—if you're going through an emotional time, ask yourself, "What is my opinion here?" You might say, "I'm insecure, Stu, because I think I might be losing my job." Okay, stop and pull back. What can you do about it? The way it is, is the way it is. You perceive that things aren't going well at work, so what's the next step? Action. Rather than running away because of emotion, like a little child who gets scared and flees, when you're faced with adversity, step forward in your feelings, not back. Write it down and put it on your refrigerator: "In challenging circumstances, I will step forward, not back." Review the situation and take action.

When there's trouble at work, what can you do to fix it? Who can you talk to, to square things away? The factory may be laying off people, but they probably won't lay off everyone, so what can you do to improve your performance? What can you do to fix the trouble? Well, first you can create more energy. But if that doesn't work, what's the worst that can happen? You're going to get chucked out of the job, and you'll find something else to do. So maybe the universe is helping to release you from one dumb job, opening up doors for you to find something more creative and more profitable to do.

Maybe when you take a long, hard look at it, it's time to chuck the job. Maybe you've been there too long. It's too crazy. You're too involved with everybody. You've lost your respect for them; they've lost their respect for you. Things get polluted if you don't watch carefully. Sometimes you have to leave and start again for people to see you in a new light.

So, emotional discipline is not buying the popular emotion, not buying into the collective ego concepts of lack, fear, insecurity—who's going to provide for me? It's not accepting the emotions that are nationalistic and warlike and staying inside that serenity that is you. You're in flow. You're in the arms of the God Force. You are the God Force. Never forget that. It's important to remind yourself that the Infinite Self is dynamic and fast-changing, and your life will begin to reflect that nature so it can rest in a perpetual state of dynamic change and not-knowing. But that won't bother you as you've learned not to hold on to things.

So when your mind rebels, saying, "We don't want anything new, and we don't want change," just step back and say, "Come, it's safe. Come." Then make it do something it hasn't done before, or change something. Now the lounge is in the bathroom. As you step to more and more energy, more and more silent power, you begin to perceive another dimension completely—a dimension beyond the contradictions of the ego, beyond desire, beyond opinion and feeling, beyond the common emotion.

Gradually, by processing emotion and understanding the psychological action involved, you realize it isn't really complex. It may seem so at first, but that's because you still belong to your emotions and opinions—you think they're yours and that they're real. They aren't—they belong to the ego. The Infinite Self cannot be insecure.

STEP 28

MENTAL DISCIPLINE

Sometimes being very intellectual is a huge spiritual disadvantage. If you are very clever, you tend to dwell in the mind. It's reasonable and pleasing to do so. It's the same as if you're very good at running—you may find yourself six hours a day on the track, enjoying your abilities.

Being very intellectual is a hindrance, but it's not the death blow to the spiritual quest. If you're not very bright, take a moment to kneel down and pray and thank God. It's a great gift to be a bit dim.

In the Tao, they revered the disadvantaged. There's a strange concept in the writings that says the tallest tree is the first one to get cut down. The crooked, gnarly tree that is ugly and bent is of no use to the carpenter, so it grows for a thousand years. The cripple doesn't have to go to war. He isn't required to perform. So, the cripple is revered the same as the gnarled, crooked tree. The Tao says,

To remain whole, be twisted!
To become straight, let yourself be bent,
To become full, be hollow....

Of course, hollow means free of stuff. If you don't have a lot of intellect, you're free, because the journey from ego to spirit is the journey from intellect to feeling. In a general sense, men deal with copious amounts of intellectuality, and less with feeling. So their journey is one out of the intellect, into feeling and beyond—into a metaphysical, spiritual perception of the world. Women, generally, are more aligned to feelings; their journey is really to quiet those feelings and go beyond their insecurity.

It's interesting that we're required to be secure in a dimension that is intrinsically insecure. The journey of the female is different from the journey of the male. The journey of the male is one of outgoing, pushing, conquering, ejaculating outwards, winning people over, selling things. The woman's journey is, generally speaking, quieter and more nurturing—that's why she lives longer. It may incorporate some of the masculine traits, but, more often that not, her spiritual trial is entering into this physical dimension in which she is often physically smaller and weaker than others. She has to develop a metaphysical, psychological, intellectual security inside a dimension in which she is intrinsically insecure. So the woman's spiritual quest is to process her feelings, especially negative ones, and become a radiant light of positivity.

The mental discipline for somebody who is very intellectual is the idea of not making your mind God and becoming arrogant. Then you have to somehow pull out of too much thinking. Excess thinking is a disease. It's what I call "over-thinking on life." When you get too mentally involved in questioning and intellectual activity, it keeps you from tapping into who you really are. You are a feeling. When you depart this earth plane, you depart as a feeling. You do not depart as 21 volumes of the *Encyclopedia Britannica*. Intellect is useful because it can earn you money and help you study; it can help you remember things. But in the end you are a spiritual being and therefore a feeling, not an intellectual concept.

Mental discipline breaks out into several different subheadings. The first is, you've got to agree to feel secure in a dimension that's intrinsically insecure. The second is, you've got to cure yourself of the disease of overthinking on life. So when you find your intellect going potty, stop it; start to push your feelings into things. That's nothing more than visualizing the circumstances, let's say, at the office, and asking yourself how it feels. How does the sales director feel? How does the campaign feel? How does my job feel?

Because the God Force permeates everything, everything gives off a feeling. Even inanimate objects give off a feeling. How does this airplane feel? Do you think I get on an airplane and just wander along in the great crapshoot of life? No way. I look at the energy of everything before I get on. I don't get on if I don't feel all right about it, even if it means I'm going to miss my appointments.

Once, years and years ago, I didn't feel good about a flight I was taking from London to Geneva. I got on anyway because I was young and unsure of my perception and because I was committed to getting there. Sure enough, going over the Alps one of the engines blew. It wasn't a life-threatening situation because we just turned around and went back to London on one engine. But we flew about an hour-and-a-half to the Swiss border, then an hour-and-a-half back to London, then we waited two hours while they dragged out another plane, and we finally made the journey down there. I should have gotten off that plane; I knew it before I got on.

So when things don't feel right, be careful. When you don't know what action to take, do nothing. Remember that, and put it on your fridge. When you don't know, don't go. And also remember when in doubt, do nowt. "Nowt" is a term from the north of

England meaning "nothing." If you don't know what to do, wait. Build energy, clean things up, organize things, seek out more information—but don't act until you know that you have to act.

Think about this. If you operate out of feelings, you're never really going to have to make any more decisions. Decision-making for most is an intellectual process. Either something feels right and you proceed, or it feels wrong and you don't proceed. Or, there is a neutral feeling, and you either don't proceed or you move very slowly and cautiously. So, either it feels right to marry Harry, and you say, "I love you, Harry; yes, I'll marry you Thursday." Or you say "No." There is no maybe. If you don't know, wait. If it feels wrong, definitely wait.

Under this discipline, decision-making changes from the intellectual turmoil of conjecture and the ego's agenda to "Hey, does it feel right?" If it feels right, proceed gingerly, carefully, and slowly. Keep asking yourself as you progress and perceive, and evaluate the results of your decisions as they manifest—does it still feel right?

If you're an intellectual person, your mental discipline is to ask yourself six times a day, "How does it feel?" "How does this taxi feel?" "How does this office feel?" "How does this cinema feel?" Look for the feeling. Bit by bit you can wrestle your subtle feelings into supporting you with their knowledge and ability so that your intellect is not dominating your life.

The intellect will suck to you ugly energy, personal criticism, and judgment; it will make you dissatisfied. You will have a triumph, and five minutes later the intellect will trash that triumph into nothing. It will show you all the things you missed out on. You made $20,000, but you could have made $24,000. The intellect likes to bitch and feel sorry for itself. If you don't control it, it will drive you nuts.

The journey from the intellect to the Infinite Self involves wrestling the intellect into stillness. Your meditation, disciplines, quiet time, and introspection are vital components. Without those, it's very hard to get the ego or intellect to back off and allow you to feel your spirituality. That spirituality is beautiful. It's enormous. It has vast energy and power, vast amounts of information.

As you seek the feelings of things, you will gradually be able to replace the intellect. You have to understand that, coming from the intellect, you're always guessing. It doesn't matter if all the graphs and charts tell you that this and that is supposed to happen. There are lots of people out there who have lost millions because of some squiggly line on a page. Previous experience doesn't necessarily describe what's going to happen next. But your feelings know.

So rather than having to go through life guessing—which is what the intellect has to do, go with your feelings. If you're already deeply in your feelings, then purify them; become stronger. Get into control of your life so that your emotions are solid. Stand silent and tall inside your feelings, and there's your discipline. Don't worry about things that are coming down the line; you won't be on that line when they show up.

So many people are fine. Their life is absolutely brilliant, but they can't bring themselves to admit it. If you look at your life, you'll probably find three, five, twenty, fifty things that are absolutely marvelous. You have a roof over your head, you have some money to spend, a nice family, nice friends, some lovely pursuits, your body is ticking along pretty good, you've got a car to bumble around in. What else are you going to need? What you need is serenity, not a bunch of mental drivel that moans and groans and makes you dissatisfied. You're with one person and you're constantly wondering if it would be better with the other person. Then you go to that person and you find it's exactly the same. Then you're off to the next one. It drives you crazy.

Too much thinking is a terrible disease. It brings on awfully chronic symptoms such as seriousness. I don't mind arrogance and self-indulgence, as I'm arrogant and self-indulgent sometimes, and I don't mind stupidity, as I've done loads of stupid things in this life, but seriousness bothers me. I flee from serious people as fast as my chubby little legs will carry me. I find seriousness close to revolting.

This life isn't serious. It's a comedy. It's an awesomely beautiful journey, but it certainly isn't serious. Serious is an egotistical concept; it comes from several factors. One is insecurity, another is self-importance, whereby insignificant people use seriousness to make themselves seem more than they actually are. Sometimes seriousness is used as a manipulation, or as a way of imposing from above on people that one considers inferior. With seriousness comes a lot of judgment and a lack of light and laughter and God Force. It's a very stony path to take.

Sometimes seriousness reflects a temperament that is less than gracious and magnanimous to others. It can be a form of intellectual snobbery. You can always tell serious people a mile off—they walk funny. The cheeks of their bum are puckered like they're holding on to a carrot. I think they feel selected by God to hold a carrot up their rear end until death. That's why you always see carrots growing near the graves of serious people. If you're too serious, start to laugh a lot; play, hang out with children, put on silly clothes, do light-hearted things and cut people a lot of slack, including yourself. Become big in your feelings, and seriousness melts in the light of your heart's newfound goodness.

STEP 29

PHILOSOPHICAL DISCIPLINE

Philosophical discipline is real simple. You have to develop a mind-set that works, one that liberates you, one that doesn't generate negative emotion and insecurity, one that doesn't involve too much control from outside. So you can read all the great writings, but the central thing about the philosophy you decide to adopt is that it should be simple.

I don't care for the sacred writings that are full of dogma, rules, and regulations. Every rule and regulation is a fence post of the prison you create for yourself. There's a huge difference between rules and disciplines. Rules are imposed from above by control freaks, the government, the IRS, the church, your family. Discipline is something you take on joyously and willingly because you know it raises your energy and quiets the mind.

Once you understand that, you'll want a philosophy that doesn't have a lot of rules. My religion is, don't have too much religion. There's nothing worse than a person who is dogmatic and full of stuff. Dogma is a manifestation of littleness. It creates tight boundaries that a little person can hide behind. Everything becomes black-and-white, simple to understand, and laced with righteousness. Everything inside the dogma fence is good, and everything outside is evil. It makes life simple by collapsing 99 percent of it.

It's a prison for the feeble. Dogma is stuff. In the enormity of the God Force, too much stuff looks silly.

I'll never forget the day I had my first experience up the other end of the near-death tube, where I actually perceived the God Force. This isn't thinking about the God Force, or a faint feeling—this is actually seeing it. The enormity of that energy is indescribable. It's exquisite beyond words. The love and compassion—there is no way to quantify and comprehend that amount of love. But what that experience did for me was to instantly throw out about 75 percent of the stuff that I believed. At the time I had my first experience of the Light, I'd been working on myself for many years, so I had already liberated my psychology and philosophy a tremendous amount. Yet standing in the light of the God Force, I felt embarrassed—a lot of my philosophy was pathetic compared to a view of the real thing.

So, move to the lightness of being. Develop a psychology that works, and stay away from pomposity and arrogance and righteousness. Avoid as much as possible talking about your philosophy to other people. Don't bother to try to win people over with your philosophy through personal arguments, and don't bother to demonstrate it. What you keep to yourself has power; what you blab about becomes less powerful. Now, it's completely different if someone comes up and asks you something. Then you can tell them what you know. But don't become a demonstrator of spiritual wonderfulness. Develop a philosophy that works, and any time a system doesn't work, take a long hard look at what you believe. Bag it if it doesn't work.

The second part of philosophical discipline is, I think, that it's important to study at least the rudiments of psychology. I don't want to intimidate you and make you think you have to go to the university and plough through endless dreary texts. But you could buy a few books on the basics of psychology, because a little knowledge really helps you understand why people act the way they act—why they do what they do.

If you study the way the mind operates, you'll understand function and dysfunction. You'll understand why people are complex and often sick. You'll understand the various psychological manifestations of man. You'll understand, for example, how transference operates in people's minds. To put it in its simplest definition: when the ego or personality feels uncomfortable, an individual will try to transfer that discomfort to someone else.

People who are psychologically crippled will tend to blame others. It's the Jewish people's fault. It's the blacks. Men are doing it to me. The wife is doing it to me. Of course, no one is doing it to you. The ego is doing it to you, and so you feel restricted. In order to get rid of that restriction, you transfer it; or you attempt to transfer it and load it up on somebody else. So discrimination is actually a manifestation of an irritated, insecure ego. That's all it is.

By looking into psychology a little bit, you understand motivations, what drives people sexually, what drives them to dysfunction and compulsion. I suggest such study because it certainly helped me in life, learning how people are going to act. Human beings, on the surface, are complex. Once you go past the surface, we're extremely simple to understand. In the tick-tock mind of the ego-personality, there are not too many urges and traits you have to learn about.

Everybody considers him- or herself incredibly unusual and different. But, in fact, 99.99 percent of all the people you're ever going to meet are, more than likely, 100 percent predictable. Even if they're acting unpredictably, what's predictable is that they'll be unpredictable. What looks like actions that are difficult to comprehend, are not so when you have a little psychology under your belt.

So, if you have a moment, pick up a book or two on psychology. There are loads in the stores, written in simple terms that describe archetypes, psychological traits, compulsions, urges, and so on. Buy the little thin ones. That's always been my policy, because it shows that the author can put his or her point across without waffling.

To wrap up philosophical discipline, the name of the game is to have as few beliefs as possible, to have little or no dogma, and as few rules and regulations as you can other than self-imposed disciplines. The best philosophy is light, breezy, flowing, changeable, accommodating, and easily forgotten. One glimpse of the God Force and 75 percent of your dogma will go out the window. On we go to Step 30—*Spiritual Discipline.*

STEP 30

SPIRITUAL DISCIPLINE

The central point of spiritual discipline is to remind yourself that you are not your physical body, emotions, intellect, beliefs, tribe, sexuality, or religion. You are an infinite being that is renting a body from the God Force. You have come to experience and transcend.

The central discipline is transcendence. What will you do today that will assist you in going beyond the physical experience and comprehending this journey better? Spiritual discipline is no more than keeping your eye on the God Force.

One exercise I recommend is, every so often when you find yourself with a quiet moment, close your eyes and visualize the divine Light hitting you in the forehead and the heart, bathing your body. Visualize it for five to ten seconds, then stop. Then do it again. You will find that, in this simple exercise, you begin to pull more and more of that infinite force into your life.

Spirituality is invisible. Never forget that. If you can see it, if it's dressed in funny robes, if it's up there to be looked at, if it's making a big performance of itself, it is not spirituality. It is ego.

Spirituality is having the Tao in your heart—to embrace the little things, to embrace the softness and the silence, the yin. It is not the act of becoming a showy person; it's the process of becoming an invisible person.

The trash man who comes around at five o'clock in the morning might have an enormous spirituality that you can't see. He is what he is; he's contained within himself. He is doing his job diligently, serving the community by hauling crud. The trash man can be an incredibly god-like figure.

Unfortunately, we tend to think that spirituality has to perform in a certain way. You could be rolling drunk in a bar and still be spiritual. Because at that moment—when you're totally sloshed out of your brain—the personality and its ego are all out to lunch, and so you're in touch with your spiritual self—but completely aligned with the God Force because your mind is gone temporarily.

So be careful that you don't get stuck in these dogmatic perceptions of spirituality. Become the crooked tree. Stand at the back. Be silent. Don't talk unless people ask you to. If you have perception, you can look at a person on the street and see their life story right there; don't say anything. If you know the answer, keep quiet; don't show it to people. If they ask you, give them a little bit, just enough to take them to the next step. But don't dump ten tons of your wisdom upon them because it isn't necessary, is it? A little bit here, and a little bit there, is all you have to do.

Basically, spiritual discipline is staying in the emanations of the God Force, believing when you can't see, knowing when you can't logically confirm it, being secure when everything around you looks insecure, being silent in a noisy world, being abundant when people tell you we're running out of everything. Stay inside that spirituality, and if you lose it, come back. Pull back. Organize. Be silent. Meditate. Pray. Take a steambath or some kind of nurturing body work. Go on a fast. Constantly purify yourself.

Be humble. People get a little bit of spirituality and then make a huge fuss over it. There's nothing more off-putting than a person who doesn't really know anything, trotting around like he or she is the sage on the mount. If you teach, teach from a distance. Teach, and then leave. But don't stay around for the applause. Be mysterious. Keep moving. Don't tell people where you are or what you know. Just give them enough to keep them moving along. That's spiritual discipline—staying with the God Force and not using your heightened power for unreasonable gain, or to keep the ego happy.

There's nothing worse than going to one of those New Age conferences and watching all those people strut about. Grim. Absolutely grim. People have such a strange idea about spirituality. They think spirituality is holy-moly, clanking little bells, putting on vestments and robes. Spirituality is the garbage man who believes in himself, the bag lady who knows who she is. She's living an uncluttered life—she's sleeping under the bridge in Central Park. That's spirituality, where you become the simplicity of the raven flying overhead, the simplicity of the little animal in the forest—at one and at peace with all things, at one and at peace with yourself.

We will now go to the last three of the 33 steps, which are *Quest, Fusion*, and *The Initiate*.

STEP 31

QUEST

Now we come to the last three of the *33 Steps to Reclaiming Your Inner Power*. These last three steps are not actually steps—they are energies or perceptions that you will align to. Step 31 is *Quest*. Step 32 is *Fusion*. Steps 31 and 32 coming together create the 33rd energy, which is *The Initiate*.

Quest is, of course, that sacred journey from ego to spirit. But it is more than that. I believe that when you make the decision to seek your Infinite Self, you are joined by a special inner energy. You can call it a guiding light, an archangel, a spiritual intuition— call it what you like.

It's almost as if in your reaching up, requesting, deciding to become more, an invisible power clicks in and joins you. There is an inner process that goes on that I believe comes from outside this planet, outside this world. From that you are suddenly joined by a very ancient, holy, very sacred energy that is older than time, which comes to allow you the ability to transcend.

In your meditations, call upon the power of *Quest* to join you, and you will feel it come into your life. It will show you things. I have great respect for it; it helps to form a bridge from this world to the inner worlds and dimensions inside the Infinite Self. It's part of the great mystery. Where it comes from I know not; it's a reservoir of energy that many never tap into properly. It's there to help.

At the end of this earth's evolution, we're all going to have to transcend, because otherwise we are going to create mayhem on the earth plane, a living hell. The final journey for everybody on this planet is to reach the point inside of themselves where they are spirit rather than ego. At the moment, we are physical bodies and egos. We're Italians, Germans, French, Africans, Asians, and whatever. In the end, we will all become spirits that happen to be in a physical body that was born in Vanuatu—or wherever you were born.

Quest is a sacred energy that you call into your life. It isn't really there for you to make more money. It isn't there for you to gain more power and have more sexual experiences. It's a sacred energy that helps you leave the emotion of this existence.

I talked to you earlier about the mystical parchment, where you've written your name down as wanting to evolve. When you made this decision to evolve, what you actually agreed to do was to kill off the ego. In other words, to evolve beyond the earth plane and remain in it is a great prize. You get all the benefits of this incredible evolution, and the beauty of it all, but you're not sucked into the agony of it. So that's your prize. But, in order to claim your prize, you've agreed to kill the ego off.

As you get into spiritual disciplines and you begin to meditate, fast, and go through all the processes we've talked about in the previous 30 steps, you begin to disenfranchise and disempower the ego. What you're really doing is *disappearing* your personality.

If, on your journey, you find that you have morbid thoughts and you feel like you're dying or falling apart, know that it's part of the process. The feelings come up because the ego's world is melting away, so it feels belittled and sad. I've had people describe it to me in my seminars as little bits of themselves falling away, like an ice floe that melts and cracks and floats away. Each bit that falls away serves to make you lighter and more spiritual; your energy grows and, with that, your perception.

In *Whispering Winds of Change,* I talked about the symbol of Christ on the cross as a poignant symbol of the death of the ego. You have to give yourself away in order to find yourself. In the story of Jesus, we see him as a great light in a human body—with a personality and ego that has to die and rise again after three days. At the foot of the cross are Mary Magdalene and the other women. This was a way of saying that while the ego is going through its death, the femininity inside of you—the yin, the softness, the silence, the Tao, the sacredness—has to just sit, watch, and wait. There's nothing it can do to save the ego, because your spirituality cannot be truly reborn until you enter in on the decision to kill off the ego.

So Jesus is on the cross for three days, and the women wait, ready to accept the death of the ego so that the Christos and the spirituality of the Infinite Self can come forth. Jesus is placed in a tomb—or in a trance state, a meditative state. It's a silent place away from the world, from materialism, from Pontius Pilate, the Romans, the followers, away from the razzmatazz or whatever showbiz was going on in Palestine at that time. He is in silence. Then after three days he rises again, accepting and embracing spirit. At that point, he becomes the Christ, the Christos, imbued with the holy spirit, transcendent.

The process for you is very much the same. Your energy will go up and you'll find yourself in the razzmatazz of personal power; you will seemingly perform miracles for people. They may want to follow you and declare you a god. But, in the end, you are killing off the ego, and you will go through your quiet time. There you retreat within the yin of the Infinite Self—the spirit within you—as it rises from its eternal silent resting and takes its rightful place. You ascend to another plane of existence. But you won't be dead; you'll still be in your body—here and not here, human and not human, beyond the pain and confusion—in a dimension of pristine clarity, with a dispassionate vision of the heroic evolution of our people.

Quest requires that you agree to the journey. Second, it asks you to understand that as you evolve you will kill off your personality. That doesn't mean that you won't have a personality, won't remember things, or won't be who you are. But you kill off the dominance of the ego-personality within you and start to see things in a completely different way. It's like taking a piece of art that's painted on a transparent kind of paper, shining a light behind it, and seeing the painting completely differently.

You're going to take the light of perception and shine it behind your day-to-day reality. As the light shines, you're going to see the world in its true evolutionary state. You will see how it actually is, not how it appears to the intellect. The process will completely transform your attitude, your emotion, your intellect, your psychology, your spirituality. It will also change your physical body. The more spiritual you become, the faster the cells of your body oscillate—which will require balance—and the faster it can heal and maintain itself as well.

Quest is that sacred moment when you kneel down with your God and say, "God, make me wise." At that point, *Quest* is there for you. Sometimes in your meditations you might see it as a hooded monk who has no face. Under his or her robes—it has no particular gender—is a brilliant light that shines but that is hidden for fear of burning you with too much energy. *Quest* is the 31st energy of the 33 Energies of Man. It comes to you as a gift when you make the initial turn.

For me, the turning point was when I started to give up my personality traits. I'm half-English and half-Sicilian. When I was a young man in my twenties, I really *did* Sicilian. I lived in urban London, and I was pretty successful in the jeans business. There were an awful lot of criminals around in those days, so I used to travel with this entourage of characters: roughnecks and bodyguards, girlfriends, assorted other people. The perfumed circus, I used to call it, because it was so Mafioso and out of control.

One day I woke up and thought, "Wait a minute. I was raised in Africa and educated in Britain. I'm not Sicilian. My name's Wilde, not Corleone. What am I doing all this for? It's ridiculous." I remember deciding to trash Sicilian. In those days, I had a black hat that I wore just about everywhere. I burned the hat, pouring a bottle of brandy over it to set it alight. That was my way of releasing being Sicilian. I think *Quest* comes when you get out of, "I'm Irish, I'm Protestant, I'm female, I'm old, I'm young...." You get out of those definitions and just realize that you are an eternal being inside a body that happened to be born in Ireland or wherever.

Quest comes at the sacred moment where you agree to quit. It's a beginning and an ending at the same time. It's that sacred moment when you agree to abandon the fight, the struggle, the emotion, the world of the ego-personality, and you step away. And as you do so, there is an absolute power that joins you from within, that assists you. It isn't going to lay out the path for you for the next 20 years, minute by minute, day by day. But it shines a light in front of you. It's like miners' lamps that shine a yard or two in front to show them the rock-face they're digging.

S T E P   3 2

FUSION

From *Quest* we go to *Fusion*. *Fusion* is somewhat hard to explain. *Fusion* is a consolidation of power. Radiating from your body is an energy that is normally not visible to the naked eye but is definitely there. The name I prefer for it is the *etheric*. Some people call it the subtle body. It is more than the causal body—it's the totality of the electromagnetic energy that flows from you, imbued with the total feeling that you are. It's not normally visible to the naked eye, but you can train yourself to see it if you can reactivate your peripheral perception.

Peripheral vision is, of course, perceived with the side of the eye. Over thousands of years, we have lost much of our peripheral perception—the cells in the side of the eye have become less aware because we don't need peripheral perception to keep us safe in the forest. You can wake those dormant cells back to life and usefulness. It's nothing more than constantly asking yourself, "What is to my left, and what is to my right?" Then look to the side without moving your eye. Doing this, you begin to activate the rods in your eyes. I'll explain.

There are two types of cells in your eyes. The ones in the center are called cones, and the ones on the outside, which are more sensitive than the cones, are called rods. Peripheral perception comes from the rods. The rods are colorblind, but they can pick up the etheric. You just have to practice. Spread your arms out on either side of you, and start moving them toward your back. Notice when they disappear from your view. Broaden your field of vision by looking at the side constantly, and over a few months, your peripheral vision starts to come back.

Let's talk a bit about the etheric. In a regular tick-tock person, the etheric is all over the place. It's flying out from them, responding to emotions and thought-forms, responding to their physical energy. It's flying around like steam. But, unlike steam, it's fast; it moves like little bolts of lightning, and they're burning energy left and right.

When you come back inside yourself, the etheric consolidates. You come back through the intellectual and emotional discipline, through physical control, through understanding yourself in an infinite sense, and suddenly the etheric is defined. That takes you away from the tribal emotion, because your energy is now not permeating other people as you're walking along. There's a defined place where you are, and that is different and distanced from where everybody else is. Now there's an etheric gap between you and the rest of the world. Fusion takes place because of that gap. The various components inside you come together, and another defined click takes place.

Right now, more than likely, your inner dialogue is contradictory and negative. I don't mean this as a criticism, but let me explain myself. Because of the insecurity and the programming we acquire in childhood, and the experiences that the personality remembers or has heard about, almost everyone has a negative inner dialogue. So someone will come up with an idea and say, "I think I'll organize a seminar in three weeks' time at the diddly-

diddly hotel." The mind says, "No good, it won't work, you'll never get the price, you can't make it work." You feel good, and the ego says you don't. It's a perpetual inner doubt.

There is a point on this journey, at the point of *Fusion,* when your *Quest* takes on critical velocity. You've processed yourself, you've worked on your emotions, you've gone through the discomfort of it all, you've gone through the process of discovering who you are. You've disciplined the mind over a period of years, and suddenly a synapse takes place. Your inner dialogue flips from negative to positive.

It's almost as if you're a magnetic field moving gradually back from one polarity to zero, and suddenly you flip to another polarity, like the magnetic energy of the earth does sometimes. At the point where fusion takes place, the flip happens. You're then more spirit than personality. You're mostly spirit, and only partially a physical body and personality. That's what Fusion is. At that moment in time, your dialogue will flip to a positive dialogue.

So you'll be walking along and thinking, "I'll put on a seminar in three weeks' time. I'm not sure if it's going to work. I wonder if we'll get enough people. I wonder what it's going to cost." Your inner dialogue will say, "It's fine. Go ahead. Do it, it will work. Invest." It will actually come forward and be totally positive. Intellectually, you might be cautious, but now the inner dialogue contradicts the intellect. It's more powerful, and it will come from a totally positive view in all things. Your intellect says, "I don't think I feel strong today," and the inner dialogue will respond with, "We're fine, drink a pint of carrot juice." There's no doubt—not the slightest hesitation or fear. The dialogue knows.

Even when the inner dialogue needs to warn you or show you that you need to adjust, it doesn't do it in a negative way. It doesn't say, "Warning, warning, fear, fear, danger, danger." It just says, "Proceed cautiously," or "Take a look at the knots in this rope prior to stepping off this cliff." You take a look at the rope and notice it's not in the carabiner. And you think, "Wow, that's good news. I'd better put the rope in the carabiner before I climb down this cliff."

Fusion is a great moment. It's that place where you experience the complete consolidation of the power, when you can stand and say, "I am what I am, and I accept that." And you mean it. It resonates eternally throughout the whole of your feelings. There is no part of you that says, "No, you're not." *Fusion* shows you an enormous world that is not normally visible. So *Fusion* follows on after *Quest* has been established. Then you are joined by another energy, a different energy, which is created by *Quest* and *Fusion* mixing and exploding together.

As I said, the 33rd energy is not a step—it's more the conclusion of this whole journey. It is the energy of *The Initiate*.

STEP 33

THE INITIATE

The energy of *The Initiate* is elusive to describe because it is beyond the mind—beyond the subconscious—and intellect. It's outside what we consider the earth's evolution. It is here and not here at the same time. Trying to put it into words and descriptions is a bit of a futile exercise—like the first words of the *Tao Te Ching*, which says that the Tao that can be defined is not the Tao. The grace of God that can be defined is not the grace of God. The spirituality that you can define is not spirituality. The philosophy that you can define is not a complete philosophy, because in the end, philosophy is a feeling as well as a concept.

The Initiate is outside of human evolution. It's beyond, in another place. Permeating this evolution here are countless other dimensions. The physical experience that we describe as humanity is one molecule, one thought-form. There are countless others. Some of them are right here. There are people walking this earth who were originally in the physical 1,000 years ago. There are energies here beyond the mind.

The 33 Energies of Man are 33 energies that make up one energy, one total energy. The way to visualize it is to imagine 33 pieces of intertwined string. As they twist around each other, they make a rope. The 33 energies are part of our evolution. They are the pathway out and the highway into this evolution. They have been here since the beginning of time; they will be here beyond the end of time because they're infinite.

As I worked on myself over the years and went through the processes that have been described in this book, the inner doorway opened for me. I began to comprehend what is truly occurring here.

What is happening is awesome. In a way, for a little human mind, it's terribly scary. But in another sense, it's terribly beautiful. For me, the decision was easy because I'd been everywhere, done everything, and if I didn't search for some other place to evolve, I was finished. More than likely, I would have projected myself out of the earth plane. I would have pulled an event to me that would allow me to end this existence. As it was, a doorway appeared. Each time I got to the end of a set of energies, a set of experiences, a set of comprehensions—just at the point where I sat down and thought, "Well, that's it, Stu, you might as well kick the bucket and go," another door clicked open.

For many of you, this is your process as well. You're done with this mundane earth-plane stuff. You're done with the crud, yet you don't need to die. What you need is the courage to evolve.

The 33 Energies of Man comprise a sacred power that isn't in books. You can't get it in a seminar. It's an understanding beyond the mind. The intellect will say that none of these worlds exist. But as you approach them, you'll know that they're there. You probably *already* know that they're there.

I remember walking in the mountains of New Mexico, close to a place called Sipapu, where every year I meet with my friends and present seminars up there high in the mountains. I was walking along a mountain track with my dog. The animal suddenly became agitated and stood rock still. Its ears pricked up as it looked across the road and up an embankment toward some fir trees. I looked up, expecting to see some little animal. Instead, what I saw was mysterious, stunning.

About 30 yards off to my right was a geometric shape, violet in color; it hovered in the air about head height, rotating in slow motion. When I say it was geometric, it was not a part of any geometry that I'm used to. It wasn't a square or a triangle or a cube or an oblong. But it had geometric proportions. It sounds contradictory, but I experienced the perception of a geometric shape, and yet I cannot explain its geometry. It's as if it existed in a 5-D world or a multidimensional state that was converted for my benefit into 3-D perception.

I watched, mesmerized, as the thing rotated. It was incredibly beautiful. It moved in a strange way—both purposeful and composed. It had serenity. It seemed to me that it had intelligence. It knew what it was doing. After a short while, my dog became satisfied that there was nothing on the embankment that it might be interested in, so it wandered off. I continued to watch the geometric shape as it hovered and turned. Suddenly, instantly, it crossed the dirt road. I had no perception of motion, of it traveling the distance that separated us. It was 30 yards away, and instantly it was in front of me.

There was no appearance of motion between the two places. It was over there, and suddenly it was hovering at head height, three feet in front of me. I didn't see it actually move between the two locations. It hovered in front of my eyes, rotating incredibly slowly. It was showing aspects of itself to me. The geometric shape was very complex, yet very beautiful; the more I looked at it, the more I saw. There were shapes inside shapes, colors inside colors. It had what I can only describe as personality. It had character—a sacredness about it—a spiritual identity. It wasn't just a mechanical diagram in motion. It was a being, a geometric being. It had an enormous spirituality, and it had a way of pulling my concentration inside its goodness.

It hovered there for a moment, then it gave me what I can only describe as a gold-colored ring. It didn't actually give it to me; it just hovered near me. The ring was about eight inches in diameter. The gold ring was a clue, a key if you like, that would unlock a door that came three years later. The ring hovered over me so that it was about 18 inches above me. The moment after it gave me the strange ring, the geometric shape leaned toward me, ever so subtly, like it was in a silent prayer or acknowledgment.

The process of it hovering in front of me, and the ring, took about 30 seconds, then it shot off to my left. I saw it cross an embankment and past a grassy area, through which a stream flowed. It hovered on the other side of the stream at about 20 to 30 feet. It hung there in the air for about eight to ten seconds, and it suddenly disappeared like a soap bubble that had burst. It was there, and suddenly it wasn't there anymore.

From that experience, I came to realize that there are many things beyond the mind that we don't understand. Since that day, I've had eight to ten more of those types of experiences, as well as seeing comparable inner visions and symbols that are a part of the ring's teachings or messages. A lot of it is way past my knowledge or comprehension. But what I find is that if I see something I don't understand, then over a period of a few years I piece it together like a jigsaw; then I understand it.

I'd go into details, but sometimes it's impossible to describe. So many of these things are indescribable. They're places that don't exist, dimensions that are moving backwards, folding inside themselves. There are beings that are here, but not here. What it all means, one day perhaps I'll know. On the other hand, most of it I'll probably never know. But in the sight of it, in the privilege of it, I learn things I don't know, and even though I may never be able to explain it all, someday, someone—you, perhaps—will.

So, as you step toward that 33rd energy as I have, the visions will guide you. *Quest* will guide you. *Fusion* will allow you to make the transcendence. Once you do step across, you're not dead. You're not finished. You're not sitting upon a mountain with a little robe on, clanking a bell, 500 followers kissing your toe. You're the garbage man—eternal, immortal, hauling garbage. Looking up the street and seeing through people like they're transparent. Being a part of those angelic dimensions. Being a part of the spirits of nature. Understanding the evolution of water and air, earth and fire. Living inside an etheric dimension, on the one hand, and being a garbage collector on the other.

If you ever come across a person who has absolutely mastered this 33rd energy, you will never know it. I know I will never master it until the day comes when I can step past teaching. Little by little over the years, I have begun to make fewer appearances; I show up in fewer places. So I'm thankful, because I'm getting there. But one day, someday, I'm going to buy a taxi, and I'm going to retire inside the world of the 33rd energy of man, if it will allow me to, that is.

I'll drive my taxi. And who will be sitting in the back seat smiling? You'll be sitting there, and you'll say, "Hello, Stu, what are you doing here?"

And I'll say to you, "I'm practicing—like you are—I'm practicing in becoming nothing."

Bless you, and may God speed your journey.

ABOUT THE AUTHOR

Author and lecturer **Stuart Wilde** is one of the real characters of the self-help, human potential movement. His style is humorous, controversial, poignant, and transformational. He has written 16 books, including those that make up the very successful Taos Quintet, which are considered classics in their genre. They are: *Affirmations, The Force, Miracles, The Quickening,* and *The Trick to Money Is Having Some.* Stuart's books have been translated into 12 languages.

Stuart Wilde International Tour and Seminar Information

For information on Stuart's latest tour and seminar dates in the USA and Canada, contact:

White Dove International
(800) 962-4457
www.whitedoveinternational.com

Stuart's Website:
stuartwilde.com

We hope you enjoyed this Hay House book. If you would like to receive a free catalog featuring additional Hay House books and products, or if you would like information about the Hay Foundation, please contact:

Hay House, Inc.
P.O. Box 5100
Carlsbad, CA 92018-5100

(760) 431-7695 or **(800) 654-5126**
(760) 431-6948 (fax) or **(800) 650-5115 (fax)**
www.hayhouse.com

Published and distributed in Australia by:
Hay House Australia Pty. Ltd. • 18/36 Ralph St. • Alexandria NSW 2015
Phone: 612-9669-4299 • *Fax:* 612-9669-4144 • www.hayhouse.com.au

Published and Distributed in the United Kingdom by:
Hay House UK, Ltd. • Unit 62, Canalot Studios
222 Kensal Rd., London W10 5BN • *Phone:* 44-20-8962-1230
Fax: 44-20-8962-1239 • www.hayhouse.co.uk

Published and Distributed in the Republic of South Africa by:
Hay House SA (Pty), Ltd., P.O. Box 990, Witkoppen 2068
Phone/Fax: 27-11-706-6612 • orders@psdprom.co.za

Distributed in Canada by:
Raincoast • 9050 Shaughnessy St., Vancouver, B.C. V6P 6E5
Phone: (604) 323-7100 • *Fax:* (604) 323-2600

Tune in to **www.hayhouseradio.com**™ for the best in
inspirational talk radio featuring top Hay House authors! And, sign up
via the Hay House USA Website to receive the Hay House online newsletter and
stay informed about what's going on with your favorite authors. You'll receive
bimonthly announcements about: Discounts and Offers, Special Events,
Product Highlights, Free Excerpts, Giveaways, and more!
www.hayhouse.com